THE CHOICE

AN EDUCATOR'S JOURNEY THROUGH UNEMPLOYMENT

BY
NANCY CHESSMAN

First published by Dog Ear Publishing
4011 Vincennes Rd
Indianapolis, IN 46268
www.dogearpublishing.net

ISBN: 978-1-4575-5942-6

This book is printed on acid-free paper.

Printed in the United States of America

This book is dedicated to Boyd, for his constant support,

and to Kayla for her unending encouragement.

PROLOGUE

I am an educator. My professional background, spanning several decades, has been spent in various schools and classrooms. I have worked with students of all ages - kindergarten through adulthood. The majority of my career, however, was spent teaching math to hormonal middle school students.

When I began writing this book, I was unemployed. I was laid off of my job in 2012, however, my journey began in 2011 when I was presented with a choice from my employer. The decision I made at that time resulted in profound repercussions for me.

There are two reasons why I decided to write this book. First, I wanted to share my journey through unemployment so others in the same situation would know they are not alone in the day-to-day ups and downs - the whole "misery loves company" thing. There are millions of people who are, or who have been, affected by unemployment. Unemployment does not just affect the person who lost the job; it affects the whole family. Being a lifelong educator, I felt a need to share my experience in hopes of helping others.

The second reason why I wrote this book was to help me. I found very early on in my writing that it was cathartic. There were times that I had to walk away from my computer as I was writing because the emotions evoked brought back so many painful memories. Throughout most of the process, though, it felt therapeutic to tell my story.

With the exception of my husband, Boyd, and my daughter, Kayla, I have changed the names of the other primary players in this story to protect the innocent (or guilty?).

* *

We've all gone through difficult times in our lives. Until the summer of 2012, I had thought the worst summer of my life was in 1978. In April of that year, my high school sweetheart of two years broke up with me. I was a sophomore in college; he was a freshman. Visiting his gay brother in San Francisco over spring break, he came out of the closet himself. I was wearing a promise ring featuring a diamond you could see only with a magnifying glass. We had already chosen names for our future children (Jennifer and Christopher, in case you were wondering).

With my future husband and children taken away from me, I spent that summer back home with my parents, working nights popping popcorn at a local outdoor theater, sleeping until one or two in the afternoon, and pretty much feeling sorry for myself the entire time. It was a depressing, lonely summer. My mom and my friends, trying to cheer me up, all felt obliged to tell me, "Nancy, we all knew he was gay." To this I replied, "I didn't! And none of you thought to share this with me?" So, as summers go, that one was the second worst I've experienced.

Another difficult time started in 2002 when my family suspected my dad was in the early stages of Alzheimer's disease. Dad was having memory issues with completing simple daily tasks and eventually recognizing familiar faces. He soon needed constant supervision, handled mostly by my mom. One by one, he forgot the names of his grandchildren, then children, and finally, his wife. Dad ended up spending the last three years of his life in a nursing home in the Alzheimer's wing. Visiting him pulled on my heartstrings: despite knowing he would not recognize me, there was always the hope that he would have a spark of memory.

Dad died in June of 2007 - the day before my birthday. We knew the end was near, and I prayed he would not die on my birthday. Being the oldest of four children, and the only daughter, I was in charge of putting the picture boards together for his funeral. That task helped me to relive all the great times our family had had over the years and to celebrate my dad's life.

In the fall of 2010, my only child left home for college. It was difficult for my husband and me to transition into being empty nesters. While we want our daughter to become a successful, independent adult, we still want to see her often. During her senior year of high school, we celebrated her last tennis match, her last concert, the awards ceremonies and graduation, all the while knowing we were losing her in a few months. Even though she has now graduated from college and is part of the working world, I still think about her, and miss her, every day.

So, to summarize, I've gone through some difficult times throughout my life; I've been able to get through those times and have grown stronger because of them. Most of us have lost our first love, a parent, maybe even a child moving away. Unfortunately, none of that prepared me for the loss of my job.

1

FULFILLING MY DREAM

I had a "Happy Days" childhood. I was the first-born followed, much to my dismay, by three brothers. We lived in a medium-sized Wisconsin city in a friendly neighborhood surrounded by the voices of childhood friends riding bikes to the pool, throwing together a quick game of baseball, or playing "Kick the Can" long after dark. We either walked or rode our bikes to school until the snow fell. Once winter hit, we carpooled to school with neighborhood friends.

If we were really lucky our parents would load the family into the station wagon and take us to the outdoor theater on a Saturday night. We would bring lawn chairs, blankets, and mosquito repellant. Mom would pop popcorn and load a cooler with sodas for us to enjoy during the movie.

Every Sunday morning we went to St. Therese Catholic Church. My parents would sit strategically between my brothers in an attempt to get them to behave. It usually didn't work. In the 1970s, when my brother and I were in high school, we sang in the church "folk group." We thought it was so cool to be singing songs by the Beatles and Cat Stevens in church. It definitely kept us interested in attending each Sunday.

Life wasn't perfect – my brothers and I did our share of fighting, dad either lost his job or quit several times before he started his own successful business – but for the most part we were all happy.

* *

Since I was a young child, I knew I wanted to be a teacher. It was an easy choice for me. I loved helping others learn and felt a great sense of satisfaction when someone I was teaching was successful. I remember playing "school" with my friends or my three younger brothers. I always wanted to be the teacher. My parents even got me a small chalkboard one year as a birthday gift. I loved using it while "teaching."

Despite warning me that I wouldn't get rich if I pursued a career in education, my parents also encouraged me to follow my dream. So after I graduated from high school, I headed to the University of Wisconsin – Madison and earned a Bachelor's Degree in Elementary Education. I couldn't wait to start teaching, however, I was unable to find a teaching job in the Madison area. I worked as a teller in a bank, but after a few months I became very bored.

With an unpromising job market for teachers in the Madison area, I decided to look elsewhere. I spent some time thinking about where in the United States I might want to relocate. After careful consideration, I narrowed my choices to Colorado, Arizona, and Texas. Colorado was on my list because our family had vacationed there while I was a teenager. It's a beautiful state, however, I eliminated that option because I really wanted to move somewhere warm. Arizona was one of my choices because of the climate and because I had relatives that lived there. I knew no one in Texas, but I'd read some interesting things about the state and knew it was warm. Ready for an adventure, I weighed the pros and cons and made a decision – I was going to move to Texas.

Back in the early 1980s, people didn't look for jobs online – there was no Internet. So in the spring of 1981, I located a list of all the school districts in Texas and got out a map. I sent letters to about 50 school districts - located in or near the bigger cities - asking them to mail me a teaching application. Soon after, the applications began arriving in my mailbox. I spent hours filling them out - by hand. It took me a month to finish the task.

By late July, I hadn't been contacted by any of the school districts in Texas, but I was determined to make the move. Plans were made for mom and me to drive down to Texas in mid-August. If nothing came up in education, I could always work in a bank again, temporarily. Miraculously, about a week before my departure, I received a phone call from a school district in San Antonio. An interview was scheduled, and I finished my packing.

I guess that job was meant to be because I nailed the interview and was offered a job as a 2nd grade teacher in an elementary school on the southeast side of San Antonio. Mom stayed with me for about a week, helping me find a reasonably priced apartment and a church. It meant so much to me, having her there for support and advice.

As my parents had warned, I was barely making enough to survive. During my first year of teaching, I made $11,100. Peanut butter and jelly sandwiches and bottled spaghetti sauce filled my cupboards because it's all I could afford. I even took a second job as a cashier in a grocery store to help make ends meet. But the pay didn't matter because I was a teacher!

Anticipating that very first day of my teaching career, I spent count-less hours putting up bulletin boards, studying the curriculum, and preparing materials. Boy, was I in for a rude awakening when school began. Nothing can fully prepare a new teacher for that first day of school. Standing alone in front of a room full of seven year old children, I realized all the college courses, even my student teaching, wasn't quite enough to prepare me for the experience. Until you've lived it, you can't fully understand what it takes to teach. The learning curve of a first year teacher goes up quickly and most realize within that first year whether they are going to continue in the field or leave it for a different career path.

As the months passed, I began to feel comfortable in my new role as a teacher. I was learning just as much, if not more than my students. I felt like I was really helping the children and began to realize that I was good at what I was doing. How great is that? I loved my job, felt fulfilled, and was helping others.

I realized rather quickly that my favorite subject to teach was math-ematics. My undergraduate degree certified me to teach through 8th grade, and I began wondering if I should teach middle school. That way I could teach math all day and teach it at a higher level. Then something happened that pushed me further in that direction.

One day, while I was working with a small reading group, one of my second grade boys came up and asked me if he could use the bathroom. I told him to wait until break time. A few minutes later, I heard someone crying in the back of the classroom. The young boy had wet his pants. I felt so bad for him and guilty for not letting him go to the bathroom. That incident was the catalyst that propelled me into switching to middle school.

Before I could teach middle school math, I needed to take several classes in order to earn a math certification, so I enrolled at the University of Texas – San Antonio. Although I continued to teach elementary school for two more years, I switched to 5th grade (the pants wetting thing really got to me!).

After teaching at the elementary level for three years, I obtained a middle school math teaching position. As fate would have it, on the first day of in-service, I met my future husband – although I didn't know it at the time. Boyd taught science at the middle school, and, after a few conversations, we realized we shared some of the same interests. Our first date was spent on a tennis court. The rest, as they say, is history.

Soon after I began teaching at the middle school, I decided to go back to UT – San Antonio to earn a Master's Degree. Perhaps money should not be the incentive to further one's education, but within the world of teaching, the only way to earn a salary increase (and a decrease in the consumption of peanut butter and jelly sandwiches) was to obtain a Master's degree. So after several years of full time teaching and part time schooling, I finally earned a Master's Degree in Education.

A couple of years after Boyd and I married, we made the decision to move about 100 miles north to Austin, Texas. Boyd wanted to take a break from teaching and was able to work with his father, who owned a construction business. I found a middle school math teaching position, and we settled down in a city we grew to love. After a few years, Boyd ended up taking over his dad's business, running it successfully for many years.

After five years of marriage we were blessed with a beautiful baby girl. Because Boyd was making more money in the construction business than he had as a teacher, I was able to stay home for a couple of years after our daughter, Kayla, was born. Although I loved being a stay-at-home mom, I decided to teach a couple of classes at Austin Community College. I taught basic math skills to adults. It was a great job – I was able to help adults who had struggled with math during high school. For the first time in my life, my students were thanking me for helping them understand math.

When Kayla was five, we moved back to Wisconsin. Boyd had only a few family members in Texas while my whole family was within 15 miles of each other in Wisconsin. We wanted Kayla to grow up close to her grandparents, uncles, aunts, and cousins. Boyd was also ready to return to teaching as owning the construction business had become very stressful.

Boyd and I were both able to find teaching jobs, middle school science and math, respectively, upon our return to Wisconsin. Kayla started kindergarten in the fall, and we were able to get together with my family quite often. We were living the American dream – we owned a home, had stable jobs, and lived in a safe, quiet neighborhood.

After teaching for a few years, I began to take on some leadership positions within the school district. I served as the Math Department Head, a Team Leader, and even presented at a national math convention. Noticing how much I was enjoying this leadership, Boyd suggested that I become a school administrator. At first I scoffed at the idea – it would mean going back to school again, and I wasn't sure I wanted to leave the classroom. I so loved working with middle school students, helping them tackle a subject that many found difficult.

Although it took awhile for the idea to take hold, I soon found myself going back to school to earn another Master's Degree – this time in Educational Leadership. Kayla was in middle school and becoming more independent, so I knew I could take the time to work on this degree. I participated in an accelerated cohort program, allowing me to earn my degree in two years. Whether it was the wisdom of maturity or the fact that I really wanted to learn, I looked forward to my classes and earned this degree for all the right reasons.

Fortunately, the year I completed my degree, the school district in which I had been teaching for ten years had a one-year elementary principal job opening. I was hired for the job! After teaching for 25 years, it was back to the elementary level for me.

I think I was more nervous on my first day of being a principal than I was as a teacher walking into that 2nd grade classroom so many years before. I was now in charge of a whole school, not just a classroom. For the first few months, I questioned myself on every decision I made. Is this the best thing for the students? How many people am I upsetting with this decision? It was all very stressful. Luckily I had several colleagues who always made time to talk to me and answer my questions.

The same learning curve rule applied to my new position, and my first year as a school principal was very enlightening. I learned not only about how to be an effective administrator, but also realized that I loved what I was doing. Mistakes were made, but I learned from each one. I also learned that as a leader, I could never make everyone happy when making decisions. As my colleagues predicted, I started developing "thick skin," a process that would have to happen if I was to be successful in my leadership position. I was a different person when that school year ended – more confident in my abilities and myself.

After my year at the elementary school, I was able to transition into a middle school assistant principal position in the same school district. How different it was being an administrator at the level in which I had taught for so many years.

As an assistant principal, the majority of my day was spent dealing with discipline issues. I spoke with students for a myriad of reasons including disrespect toward teachers, stealing, and bullying. Having worked so many years with this age group, I felt confident in my discipline methods and the consequences I gave. I also became very comfortable speaking with irate parents! It was amazing how many parents blamed the school for their child's bad behavior and never once considered that their child may have done something wrong.

Much of my success during my time at the middle school was due to the help of the associate principal, Hallie. An administrator at the school for several years who was familiar with many of the students and their families, Hallie was always there for me, answering questions and giving me insight on teachers, students, and parents. She was my rock, and we became close friends.

Hallie also had a brilliant sense of humor. I remember being in Hallie's office while she was disciplining a student for some minor infraction. The student had obviously not spent much time in front of the mirror before he came to school because he had a tuft of hair sticking straight up on the back of his head.

At one point during Hallie's discussion with the boy, she asked, "Sam, have you ever watched "Little Rascals?"

"No," Sam replied, with a questioning look on his face.

At that moment, I realized that Hallie was making a reference to Alfalfa. I looked at her, she smiled, and I had to turn my head so Sam wouldn't see me almost lose it. I struggled to hold in my laughter as Hallie continued to question Sam about Little Rascals.

In my first year at this level, I witnessed my first fistfight. During my daily lunch duty in a cafeteria too small for comfort but too large for complete control, two boys began verbally accosting each other. They were standing face-to-face, yelling at each other, their insults and volume escalating as attention shifted to the confrontation.

As I approached, I heard one boy angrily yell, "You smashed my sandwich!"

"No, I didn't!" the other boy screamed.

By the looks on their faces, this fight was about more than just a smashed sandwich. Despite my best efforts at calming them down, it was obvious that neither of the boys wanted to walk away without getting physical. One of the boys threw a punch, hitting the other square in the jaw. I don't think I'll ever forget the sound of that fist connecting with the boy's face.

In our leadership training we were taught to never try to break up a physical fight. We were to use our voice, instead of our bodies, to get the students to stop. I used my walkie-talkie to call for backup, then shouted, "Boys! Stop!" Perhaps my command sounded lame, but it's about all I could do short of physically interceding and getting hit myself. When kids are swinging, they are not paying a whole lot of attention to what, or who, they are swinging at.

After each had landed a few solid hits, the fight ended. By that time Hallie was on the scene, and we each took a boy and headed for our separate offices. Unfortunately, that was only the first of many fights I would be dealing with over the next few years.

My assistant principal position lasted only two years. In a time of budget cuts, administrative restructuring took place, which eliminated my position at the middle school. The restructuring opened up an associate principal position at the high school, and I was told I would be changing positions once again. I'd like to think that my employer felt confident in my abilities to transition and knew I could handle a third school in only four years. Whether or not that was the case, it was stressful knowing I was moving to yet another school. Although I knew a few people at the high school, I had never worked at that level before. I would have to get to know another whole group of people, work with a different administrative team, and deal with high school students. Frankly, that age level scared me!

So with much trepidation, I packed my things and moved into my new office at the high school. I spent the summer months getting to know my new administrative team and soon realized that I fit right in. They made me feel welcome from the start and helped me with all my questions and concerns. Several teachers stopped by my office to welcome me, which also made me feel like I belonged.

As the first day of school approached, my nerves began to escalate again. Although I felt welcomed by the adults in the building, I had never worked as an administrator with high school students. I had heard stories about fights, cigarettes, and even drug possession and was anxious about dealing with these issues; issues that made wetting one's pants seem much more manageable!

Once school started, I realized that my fears about dealing with students at this level were unfounded. I soon learned that speaking with these young adults was very fulfilling. When a student was in my office, I was able to not only speak to him about his behavior, but also about his grades, credits, and graduation. This was very different than dealing with middle school students who routinely stated, "My grades in middle school don't count, so why should I care?" High school students knew that their grades mattered, so I had more valid talking points. I truly cared for the students and their success in school.

As expected, I experienced some major discipline issues while working at the high school. I carried out many locker and backpack searches. Cigarettes, marijuana, pot pipes, and condoms were all too often confiscated from places teenagers didn't seem to think we would look. There were also fights that I either witnessed or dealt with after the fact.

I remember an incident in which it was reported to me that a student had cigarettes visible in his car in the school parking lot. The student, a junior, was called to my office.

"Brad, I understand that you have cigarettes in your car," I stated, getting straight to the point.

A look of shock came over his face. Brad replied, "Those are my dad's cigarettes, I swear! I drove his car to school today! Am I going to get in trouble?"

As we walked out to the car, I asked Brad if he smoked.

"No, it's a disgusting habit!" he replied. "I've tried to talk my dad into quitting, but he's addicted."

When we arrived at Brad's car, indeed, the cigarettes were in plain view. I had Brad open the door and asked him to give me the cigarettes. Back in my office, I called Brad's father, putting him on speakerphone. He verified that the cigarettes belonged to him and that Brad did not smoke. I informed both Brad and his father that school rules dictated a one-day suspension for a first-time cigarette offense.

After I disconnected from the phone call, it was apparent that Brad was upset and embarrassed. He was a good kid who had not been in trouble before. In an attempt to bring levity to the situation I said, "Next time you drive your dad's car to school, at least hide his cigarettes in the glove box!" That put a smile on Brad's face.

Luckily, the cigarettes, drugs, and fights were not daily occurrences. I had many opportunities to connect with students in a positive way. At times I felt like a counselor or even a mom, but more than ever, I knew I was helping students in many ways. Every day was different and I loved going to work.

* *

Being a school administrator was a different kind of fulfilling. I was not only helping students but also teachers, support staff, and parents. I was able to reach so many more people than I did in my math class-room. Collaborating with a team of administrators, for the good of the students, gave me a great sense of satisfaction. During the 2010-11 school year, I was in the best place I'd ever been as an educator. I loved my job, the people with whom I worked, and to top it off, I was making a difference in the lives of many students and other educators.

Then the bottom dropped out of my world...

2

APRIL 2011
THE CHOICE

Federal Unemployment Rate: 9.0%

O n a Friday afternoon toward the beginning of April 2011, I was beckoned to the superintendent's office. Any time a staff member is asked to meet with the superintendent, anxiety ensues. Did I do something wrong? Did a parent complain about me? Whatever the reason, I left my office at the high school and apprehensively drove to the central administrative offices.

Our superintendent, Maude, was in her second year in the district. In her first two years she had already made several big changes in the district; some welcomed by staff and the community, some not so welcomed. By 2011, I had worked in the district for 14 years, having been hired by a different superintendent. Since associate principals did not attend the monthly administrative meetings, instead providing leadership in our respective buildings while our principals were out, I hadn't had all that much interaction with our relatively new leader.

One thing I did know about Maude was that there were a growing number of people who felt as if they had to tiptoe around her. She had plans she wanted to implement, and if staff did not agree with her, she was not afraid to let them know how she felt.

I remember when one assistant superintendent learned that his opinion, and expert teachers' opinions, didn't matter when Maude decided to offer advanced high school classes at the middle school. She wanted it implemented and, despite much argument against it, the program was put into practice. When Maude wanted something, she did whatever it took to get it done, no matter the opinions of her subordinates.

Due to this, and many other incidents, the entire atmosphere in the central administrative offices had changed. When walking into the building, the tension was clearly in the air. Everyone was constantly on edge, attempting to stay off of Maude's bad side.

Upon entering Maude's office, I noticed that one of the assistant superintendents, Troy, was also present in the room. That did nothing to calm my fears. With my stomach doing somersaults, I took a seat at the conference table. My throat was so dry I could barely swallow. I quickly thought, "Is this going to be good news or bad?" but I already knew the answer to that question. Good news was usually delivered in person at your school. Bad news was given in their territory.

Maude opened the conversation by saying, "The reason I wanted to talk to you today is because the district is going to do more administrative restructuring."

My first thought was "OK, so they're going to move me to another school again. I've done it before so no big deal."

That was not the message.

Maude looked me straight in the eye and continued, "For reasons that I cannot share with you today, your position at the high school is being eliminated."

At this news, my head began to ache, and I wondered if they could hear my heart pounding in my chest. A hundred questions entered my mind, but I kept quiet until the news was completely delivered.

"As you know, you have a two-year administrative contract that terminates at the end of next school year. I am giving you two options. You can remain in your current position as a high school associate principal until your contract runs out in a year, but with no guarantee of employment after that, or move into a teaching position in the fall with continued job security."

I stared at Maude, stunned. There was a buzzing noise in my ears, yet I was able to ask, "Would I be able to teach middle school math next year if I returned to the classroom?"

"At this time there are no middle school math vacancies. We do have two 5th grade openings at two of our elementary schools. You can choose which school you would like to teach at."

My heart sank. I hadn't taught at the elementary level in over 20 years. How would I ever decide what to do? In my mind I immediately began to weigh the pros and cons of each situation. Maude told me I could take up to a week to discuss it with my husband (who taught in the same school district) and make my decision.

Seeing how upset I was becoming, Maude said, "If you'd like to go home for the rest of the afternoon, that will be alright."

"No," I replied. "I'm ok to go back to school."

"Do you have any questions at this time?" Maude asked, continuing to stare at me with her steely eyes.

I tried to formulate a clear response despite the whirlwind of concerns forming in my mind and the growing angst in my gut.

"Will I be considered for any other administrative positions that might open up?" I asked.

"I cannot make any promises at this time." Maude started to shuffle some papers on the table. She clearly was finished with her end of the conversation and was ready for me to leave.

Although she had mentioned this earlier, I had to ask, "Will there really be no guarantees of employment if I remain in my current administrative position for one more year?"

"No guarantees," Maude said flatly.

My next thought I kept to myself. Does 14 years of service to the district mean anything? Obviously the answer to that question was a resounding "no."

I looked at Troy. He had said nothing during the meeting. Our eyes met, then he looked down at the paperwork in front of him. Looking back to Maude, I received an emotionless stare.

Up until that point I had been able to keep my emotions in check. When I understood that my service, my dedication and loyalty to the district really meant nothing, I broke down. I felt like I'd been punched in the gut. Depending on my decision, there was a chance that I would be laid off at the end of the next school year. People across the country who have put in many years of service at their workplace were being let go daily. That rarely happened in education, but there was a possibility that it could be happening to me.

I left Maude's office in tears, letting Troy and her know I was, indeed, going home. The drive home was methodical, my confusion and devastation demanding all of my attention. What had I done to deserve this? During the conversation Maude had reassured me, several times, that the situation had nothing to do with my job performance; I had received exemplary evaluations from my supervisors over the years. My brain just couldn't comprehend what had just happened.

When I got home, I replayed the meeting in my head over and over. My husband would be home in a couple of hours and the thought of telling him filled me with dread. This choice I was being forced to make would be a collaborative one with Boyd. Whatever the decision, it would change our lives.

* *

When Boyd arrived at home, he could tell something was wrong. My red, puffy eyes let him know that I had been crying. He sat down immediately and I explained to him what had taken place that afternoon. His first reaction was anger. The question I had asked myself earlier was spoken by him, "What did you ever do to deserve this?"

After we discussed the situation some more, Boyd's anger turned to compassion. I knew he felt tremendously sad for me and what I was going through, and always being quick to help in difficult situations, he could do nothing except be there for support. We talked for hours about the positives and negatives of remaining in my current position or taking a teaching position. Even after we stopped talking about it, we were both thinking about the future of my employment with the district.

I actually went back to school that evening when I knew no one would be around. I cleaned off my desk and brought my laptop and some work back home with me. Thinking back on that, I wonder why I bothered. But then, that's who I am. I was not going to let this devastating news impact my job performance.

We tried to watch some television that evening, however, neither one of us was able to concentrate. We kept bringing up the subject we both wanted to forget. Since no reason had been given as to why my position was being eliminated, we began speculating what was being planned by our school district. We came up with several possibilities, but none made sense. We figured we would find out soon enough. Sleep eluded us that night, both of us tossing and turning throughout the long, dark hours.

Over the course of the next few days, I thought long and hard about my options. I really did not want to go back into the classroom as a teacher – especially since it was going to be at the elementary level. I had taught only mathematics for so many years and a return to an elementary classroom would mean teaching all subjects. I also thought about what it would be like facing other teachers in the district if I did return to the classroom. I figured that the embarrassment would pass after some time, but it still wasn't something I looked forward to experiencing. Certainly, pride was influencing my decision, but then working with teachers I had once supervised would be difficult.

Another concern entered my mind when considering a return to teaching: how would that look on a resume when I began looking for another administrative position? It's something that would definitely raise a red flag with a prospective employer. I never considered the red flag that would go up if my resume reflected 15 years in the same school district and then no job at all.

There were only two positives I came up with for taking the teaching position. First, I'd be helping 25 to 30 students learn and become prepared for middle school. Second, and more importantly for my family, it would be job security.

When considering whether to remain in my current associate principal position at the high school, so many positives came to mind. First, I absolutely loved my job. I was working with a dedicated, hard-working administrative team. We got along splendidly. We worked hard and laughed hard - you have to when you work at a high school of over 2200 students.

Then there were the students and staff. I felt like I was really making a difference in the lives of the students with whom I worked. I had several "repeat offenders" who frequented my office more than once a week. Those students knew they could come in any time to vent, confide, or just talk. Staff members also felt comfortable confiding in me and knew that if they came to me with a question or a task, I would follow through as quickly as possible.

I was also involved in the development and implementation of several programs at the high school. Although I knew I wasn't indispensable, I wanted to carry out the programs in which I had become personally involved.

I thought about all these things constantly. When I returned to work on Monday, Debra, my principal called me in to let me know she was aware of the situation. We discussed some of the things I was pondering, which was helpful. I also talked to my mom about the situation. As always, she was a good listener and didn't push me in one direction or the other. She knew I'd eventually make the best decision for me.

Another outlet I had was prayer. I was raised a Catholic and while I was growing up, my family attended church every Sunday. I find it easy to pray and believe that things happen for a reason. I also believe that God has a plan for each of us and that this choice I was presented with was part of His plan. I prayed about this numerous times each day and although I wasn't given a sign or an answer, I felt confident that whatever my decision, it was what God wanted me to decide.

Before the week was over, I had made my decision. I scheduled an appointment to see the superintendent. This time it would be me delivering the news.

* *

Meeting with Maude the second time was not as stressful as the initial meeting. I brought a typed page of notes, which included the reasoning for my decision. I talked for about 20 minutes, referring to my notes and explaining my thought process. She listened intently without comment. Finally, I gave her my decision.

"I have decided to remain in my current associate principal position at the high school," I told Maude with a confident tone.

Her eyebrows raised and she said, "That's a bold move. A move I might make."

I wasn't really sure how to interpret that response. Was she comparing my decision to one she might make? Was she telling me I made a good choice?

The bottom line is that I made the choice to stay in the job that I loved, even though there would be no guarantees for the future. Part of my decision was based on the fact that I knew there might be one or more administrative openings in the district in the next year or two. I also knew that I had two cycles to look for other employment, if necessary, the current summer and the following summer.

I left the meeting feeling like a weight had been lifted off my shoulders. I felt confident that I had made the best decision for my family and myself.

Within two months, I realized I might have made a big mistake.

3

MAY 2011
THE SECRET IS OUT

Federal Unemployment Rate: 9.0%

About six weeks after I had given my decision to Maude, a meeting was called for all the administrators in the district. Having heard there would be an announcement made about administrative restructuring, I figured that one item on the meeting's agenda would be the change in my status. I also hoped that we would find out what other changes were being made that caused my position to be eliminated.

Up until that point, no one at the high school except Debra and I knew about my situation. I had been asked not to share the news with anyone else, and I hadn't. It had been very difficult for me to carry on as if nothing had changed for me. The other associate principals and I talked every day, but they had no clue what they were about to hear.

The day before the meeting was to take place, Troy, the assistant superintendent, showed up for our weekly high school administrators' meeting. Due to the fact that the announcements that were going to be made at the superintendent's meeting directly affected the high school, he wanted to give us all a heads up on what would be shared. He told us that the current middle school principal, James, was being moved to the high school the following year as an associate principal.

Shock set in. They were demoting James. Trying to not show the shock on my face, my first thought was, "What did he do to deserve this?" That was the same question I had asked myself after my initial meeting with Maude. I had worked with this man for many years, first when I was a teacher, and then as an administrator. I looked up to him as a mentor; in fact, he had been awarded "Middle School Principal of the Year" in our state the previous year. It didn't make sense.

Troy proceeded to inform our group that the Board of Education had approved the addition of an extra associate principal at the high school for one year. I knew that this had been done because of my decision to stay. I realized immediately that I had thrown a monkey wrench into Maude's plans by remaining in my position for another year.

They thought I would cave! They assumed I would choose to teach rather than to risk losing my job. When I decided to stay on as a high school administrator, Maude had to come up with another plan. She had gone to the Board of Education with some story as to why we needed a fifth administrator at the high school – and they had approved it. No wonder it took six weeks between the time I let them know my decision and the surprising announcement about James.

After hearing the news about a one-year administrative addition, I knew that my colleagues were thinking, "What's going to happen to James after next year?" But it wouldn't be James leaving the high school – it would be me. And that is precisely what Troy shared next - the fact that after next year, I would not be an administrator at the high school. I could see the barely hidden shock on my friends' faces. They couldn't believe what they had just been told. They looked at me with questioning eyes as I lowered mine.

After Troy left the meeting, my colleagues had many questions.

"How long have you known about this Nancy?" one asked.

"About six weeks," I answered, letting my eyes fall to my coffee cup.

"What? I can't believe you were able to keep it from us for that long!"

"What are you going to do after next year?" Max's eyes shifted from me to Debra and back again.

I had no answer for that question, so I just shrugged my shoulders. My throat began to tighten, once again on the verge of tears.

My colleagues seemed to be more surprised at the fact that I was leaving than the fact that James was coming to the high school in the fall. After developing such a great working relationship as well as friendship, they were clearly disappointed that I would no longer be a part of the team. When I tried to speak, my voice quivered, so I just remained silent.

The next 14 months were going to be very difficult.

When I got home that evening, I told Boyd what I had learned that day. At the meeting we had been told to not share the information because James would be informing his staff in two days. Although Boyd worked at the middle school, I needed to tell him. This so profoundly affected our lives, and I knew he wouldn't say anything to anyone. He hadn't shared my other news with anyone, and I trusted him to keep this information to himself for two days.

* *

Like many people who are under undue stress, I soon began experiencing health issues. For several years I had suffered from pain in my right hip and groin. Over the past six months the pain had increased so much it was affecting my work. I had a difficult time standing for extended periods of time, and, without realizing it, had developed a limp when I walked. Our high school was huge; a walk from one end to the other spanned a quarter mile. With my office located on the south end of the building, I walked several miles each day. Teachers, familiar with my hip pain, would wince when they saw me walking down the hall.

Throughout that year, I had seen several doctors, tried two months of physical therapy, and had even seen a chiropractor for a couple of months. Nothing was relieving my pain. I was taking ibuprofen daily, but it barely gave me any relief. I finally went to an orthopedic doctor who immediately brought up the subject of a hip replacement. In an effort to avoid major surgery, I asked if there was anything that could be done first. He suggested a cortisone shot.

Boyd has had numerous cortisone shots, and I immediately remembered his painful description of the process. Nonetheless, I was in so much pain I was willing to try anything. So we scheduled the shot, and soon after I found myself lying on a table, surrounded by equipment and medical personnel. I vaguely remember the pain of the needle deeply penetrating my hip, but it was over rather quickly.

Unfortunately, the cortisone shot did little to relieve my pain. When I went back to visit the orthopedic doctor again, we decided more had to be done. I was having groin pain as well as hip pain, so the doctor recommended "exploratory" surgery. There was a possibility that I had a hernia and that would be the only way to find out.

Like most people who are dedicated to their jobs, when I scheduled my surgery, I had to look carefully at my school calendar. I didn't want to put it off until summer because I was the administrator in charge of summer school, and I really needed to be there. That meant I would have to do the surgery in May and would miss almost two weeks of school. I also had to schedule it around all the awards programs that occur in mid to late May. As it turned out, I was able to schedule the surgery so I would only miss one of the programs.

* *

Kayla finished her freshman year of college at UW-Milwaukee in mid May. We moved her out of the dorm and back home for the summer. She was going to return to her job as a cashier at Kohls, a local department store. This is a job she had landed while in high school. She would also work, for the fourth summer in a row, at one of the elementary schools in our school district as the Summer School Secretary. I was glad she had returned home before my surgery. Since Boyd was still in school, Kayla would be assisting me during my recovery.

On May 18, accompanied by my mom and Kayla, I went in for my exploratory surgery. As I was regaining consciousness in the recovery room, the doctor came in with the prognosis. He had not found a hernia, but he had removed three inflamed lymph nodes. He was going to have them checked for cancer, but felt optimistic that they were benign. He hoped that the lymph nodes had been causing my groin pain. Time would tell.

I spent the next two weeks at home taking it easy, letting Boyd and Kayla wait on me. At my follow up appointment, the surgeon let me know that the lymph nodes were not cancerous, and I was given the ok to return to work on May 31, the Tuesday after Memorial Day. Regretfully, the pain in my groin was not gone. I hoped it was because I was still healing from surgery.

Upon my return to school, I was welcomed back by my administrative colleagues, the staff, and the students. I took it easy on my first day back, trying to limit my walking. The following day, I woke up feeling sick to my stomach. I felt like I might vomit, but then started to feel a bit better. I couldn't call in sick; I had just missed almost two weeks of school. Hoping it would settle my stomach, I ate a small bowl of cereal.

When I arrived at school, I found out that an impromptu meeting had been scheduled for the administrators. We were to meet in Debra's office at 8:00. My stomach began acting up again as I walked slowly to the meeting. When I got to the main office, several of the administrative assistants commented that I looked pale. I let them know that I wasn't feeling well. I entered Debra's office and sat down in the nearest chair I could find. My stomach was churning.

Debra's assistant came in, along with the school nurse. One of them handed me a wastebasket - just in case. That was a smart move because soon after that I threw up my breakfast into the wastebasket. After I vomited I felt a bit better, but not much. One of my colleagues ended up driving me home. I felt so guilty; it was only my second day back, and I was leaving again.

When I got home, I went immediately to bed. The pain in my stomach was not getting better, it was getting worse. Kayla heard me moaning in pain and came in asking if she could get me anything. She brought me a 7Up to sip on, just like we always did for her when she felt sick. The soda did not help the pain in my stomach. After about an hour Kayla said, "Mom, I'm taking you to the emergency room. I've never seen you this sick before." I argued for a bit but then realized that she was probably right. Something was wrong, and I needed to find out what.

Driving to the emergency room, Kayla called Boyd to let him know what was happening. Much to my dismay, I had to half-sit, half-slump in the waiting room for almost an hour before I was admitted to a room. That was the longest, most uncomfortable hour I had experienced since

I had gone through labor with Kayla almost 20 years prior.

After many questions, I was given something to settle my stomach. When that medicine kicked in, it was a tremendous help. The pain wasn't gone, but it was tolerable. As is the case in emergency rooms, things moved very slowly. Several tests were performed, and, finally, the doctor came to a possible diagnosis - appendicitis. In order to verify this, I needed to get a CT scan. Before that, however, I was told I had to drink two big glasses of lemonade-flavored medicine. Fortunately, my stomach handled all that liquid; at least for the moment.

I made it through the CT scan without throwing up, however, my stomach was starting to churn again. When I got back to my room I barely had time to grab the nearest wastebasket. All the liquid I had drunk came right back up – some in the wastebasket and a lot on the floor. I felt so bad for the nurse who had to clean it up.

Now late afternoon, Boyd came straight from school to the ER. The doctor confirmed that, indeed, I needed to have my appendix removed. The surgeon would be there shortly, but the operation would not take place until 8:00 p.m. I had Boyd call Debra to give her the update.

Since I'd be in surgery and then spending the night in the hospital, we sent Kayla home. She had spent the majority of the day with me in the ER and needed a break. Before she left she made sure to give me an, "I told you so."

Thanks honey.

* *

When I awoke after my appendectomy, the first thing I noticed was that there was no more pain in my abdomen. After suffering for almost 14 hours, the lack of pain was so very welcome. I felt terrific – and hungry. Sadly, I was restricted to a liquid diet that evening, so at 10:00 p.m. I had some chicken broth and a glass of juice.

Boyd stayed for a while, but it was after 10:00, and he had to teach the next day. Assuring him that I would be fine, I sent him home. I couldn't believe that exactly two weeks after my exploratory surgery, I had undergone an appendectomy. I wondered whether the first surgery had caused the infection leading to the second surgery. No matter the reason, I was about to miss another week or more of work. Guilt filled me once again. I would be missing the last week of school. There was also a chance I might miss the graduation ceremony.

The thought crossed my mind that this could potentially look bad to Maude. She would ultimately be the one determining my fate a year from now.

The following day when the surgeon came to visit me, he let me know that my surgery had gone very well. He told me that if I had waited much longer, my appendix would have burst. I made a mental note to thank Kayla again for insisting I go to the emergency room. The doctor gave me a color picture of my infected appendix just before it had been removed. I am very squeamish about internal body parts - especially MY internal body parts - so when I saw the picture, I could hardly look at it; however, I kept it to show my family and the rest of my administrative team. I couldn't wait to gross them out!

I asked the doctor whether I would be able to attend graduation, which was about a week away. Due to the length of time I would have to stand, he highly recommended that I not attend. Although this second surgery was a surprise, and not any fault of mine, I felt awful. I was really looking forward to attending the graduation ceremony, but it looked as if it may not happen.

4

JUNE 2011
REALITY REARS IT'S UGLY HEAD

Federal Unemployment Rate: 9.1%
Total Number of Jobs Applied For: 2
Total Number of Interviews: 0

As it turned out, I missed graduation. I was very disappointed since this was my first year at the high school. Thankfully, the ceremony was recorded and streaming live, so I was able to watch all the festivities while relaxing in my recliner. It was a bittersweet experience. I wanted to be there to support the students, but I knew that Maude and Troy were there. I was still so hurt and confused that I was having a hard time being in close proximity to Maude, and even Troy. When it was Maude's turn to speak, I muted the sound on my computer. Even the sound of her voice was enough to make my blood run cold.

****

The morning after graduation was the high school's annual Retirees Breakfast. All current and retired staff was invited for a continental breakfast, awards, and camaraderie. Any staff members who were retiring that year were given an opportunity to speak.

My doctor had given me permission to return to school that day if I promised to take it easy. I really wanted to be there because it was the teachers' last day before summer break. I hadn't seen many of them for several weeks and wanted to be able to say goodbye before they all left for the summer months.

As I walked slowly toward the cafeteria, I noticed that many people had already gathered there. As I entered the room several people spotted me and started clapping. This caught the attention of the rest of the crowd. Soon everyone was applauding; several people even shouted, "Woo hoo!" I was filled with such gratitude; I knew that people appreciated me at the high school. Unfortunately, I felt zero appreciation from my superiors.

As I walked toward the tables filled with food, I noticed Maude standing off to the side of the room talking with Debra. She had seen the reaction from the high school staff when I had walked in the room. I knew it wouldn't make any difference; however, I was glad she had witnessed the ovation directed toward me. Needless to say, I steered clear of her during the breakfast.

* *

Summer school began the following week. Since I was the administrator in charge of everything related to summer school, the courses were held in classrooms on my end of the building. On the first day of classes, I stood in the hallway greeting students and answering questions.

I thoroughly enjoyed being at school during the month of June. There were only a few dozen students attending classes, so it was relatively quiet. It was a good time to get caught up on projects that had not been completed during the school year.

Along with the slower pace came more time for my mind to wander. Deep down I knew that I should probably begin applying for jobs outside of my current school district, but that thought brought with it a feeling of dread. Even though I felt no appreciation or respect from the central office administrators, I didn't want to work in another district.

I was still holding out hope that if I did an excellent job during summer school and the upcoming year, they would consider me for another administrative position in the district. It felt as if I was on an emotional roller coaster. At times I ascended to the top of a hill, feeling hopeful about my future. Sadly, the next moment I crested the apex, plunging toward the earth. My thoughts and emotions were all over the place, uncertain of what the future held for me. The only thing I was sure of was that God had a plan for me and I needed to be patient. Easier said than done!

* *

June 2011 brought with it a milestone for Boyd and me. On June 14 we celebrated our 25th wedding anniversary. Many couples will take a trip or go on a cruise to celebrate such a big milestone. Our celebration took place at a high school baseball playoff game. All of the high school administrators were expected to attend the big game as support for the team as well as to chaperone the crowd. Because it was our anniversary, Boyd came with me to the game.

When we arrived at the baseball stadium, we headed toward the bleachers containing our team's fans. We spotted several central office administrators in attendance, including Maude and Troy, talking with my high school colleagues. Normally we would have sat by the other high school administrators, joking and having a fun time, but not tonight. I could not bring myself to be near Maude. I did not want to look at her or speak to her. So, we opted to sit by ourselves.

Our team ended up losing the baseball game. Boyd and I left as soon as the game was over, which was starting to become a pattern. We knew the others were going out for a few drinks, but we were not up to socializing with that group. Unfortunately, my future unemployment had already begun affecting my relationships, my mood, and my confidence in myself.

* *

Due to James' move to the high school, an administrative opening was created at the middle school. I didn't apply for that job for two reasons. First, I didn't really want the position. I wanted to get a few more years of administrative experience as an associate before I tackled a middle school principal position. Second, I really didn't think the district would consider me for the job.

Although there were candidates within the district that applied for the principal position, the job was ultimately given to an external candidate. She was an experienced administrator coming from a rather large school district.

Shortly after the new middle school principal had been hired, Hallie, the associate principal, accepted a job in another school district. She had applied for James' principal position and had been snubbed. Once again, Maude had turned down a highly qualified candidate.

"What is Maude thinking?" I asked Boyd soon after the news broke. Neither of us knew what was going on in her mind, or what her plans were for the school district. Actually, quite a few teachers and administrators in the district were wondering the same thing. Many feared that the outcome would be grim.

Having worked with Hallie for two years, I knew she had been looking for another job, so her move to another district was no surprise to me. Knowing Hallie might be leaving had been a factor in my decision to stay on as an administrator.

I immediately conveyed my interest in that position to Troy, who supervised the secondary schools. I requested a meeting with him to discuss the possibility of me sliding back into the middle school associate position. If I landed the position, I'd have job security once again.

My thinking in this situation was that with a new principal in the building, having an associate who had worked at the school before - was familiar with the staff and students, and who knew the ins and outs of the programming, schedule, etc. – would be the most logical decision. Many of the middle school teachers actually assumed I'd be coming back for the same reasons I just mentioned. Hallie even spoke with Maude, recommending me for the position.

On the day of my meeting with Troy, I parked off to the side of the administration building. I entered through a side door, doing everything in my power to avoid walking past Maude's office. I did not want to have any encounter with her. It would mean plastering a fake smile on my face and pretending everything was great in my life.

With confidence, I entered Troy's office. I informed him about my interest in the middle school associate principal position. Looking him in the eyes, I spelled out the reasons why I thought I would be the most qualified person to take over the job, including my familiarity with the staff and programming and the fact that I would be an asset to the new principal.

Troy's response blindsided me. He put down the pen he had been holding and said, "Nancy, the district wants to go in a new direction at the middle school. With James moving to the high school, Hallie leaving the district, and a new principal on board, we want a fresh start."

"But I would be a great resource for the new principal," I responded. "And staff members would feel comfortable having a familiar face in the office."

Nodding his head as if he understood my talking points, Troy looked me in the eye. He then reiterated that the district wanted to go in a new direction. In other words, Nancy, forget about it, you're not going to be considered for that job. It was at that moment that reality hit me – and hit me hard.

When I left that meeting, there were no tears, just a horrible feeling in the pit of my stomach. I had been kicked in the gut once again. I couldn't comprehend why something that made so much sense wasn't even being considered. I understood wanting a new direction, a fresh start. And with a new principal in place that would surely happen. Associates definitely have a voice in decisions made at a school, but the final decision is the principal's. It seemed to me that the transition would be smoother for the new principal, the staff, and the students, if I returned to the middle school. But that was not their plan.

As I drove back to school, I wondered whether the whole "new direction" explanation was something Maude or Troy concocted. I'm sure Maude knew I was meeting with Troy. Since they obviously did not want me in that position, they had to come up with a reason why I would not be considered. Anger welled up inside of me. At that moment I hated Maude for what she was doing to me.

My thoughts moved to my friend, Hallie. After working as a middle school associate principal for almost ten years, she had applied within the district for the principal position, and also a central office administrative position. Although she was qualified for both, she had not even been considered. She had been told that "she was not right for the position." Those incidents had caused her to apply to other districts. She had landed a job in her new district almost immediately.

Boyd and I speculated that Hallie might intimidate Maude. Hallie was intelligent, strong-minded, and respected by others. She was not afraid to speak the truth, even if it made people uncomfortable. I believed that I shared some of the same characteristics as Hallie. Boyd and I wondered if Maude was trying to get rid of Hallie and me because strong women daunted her. The thought that Hallie or myself could intimidate Maude was laughable. Neither one of us, however, was laughing.

The school district ended up hiring a teacher from the high school to fill the associate principal opening at the middle school. This teacher didn't even have his administrative certification yet – he was still over a year away from completing it. When I heard about this decision, I felt physically ill. They chose a person with no administrative experience and without the necessary certification for a position I had successfully navigated for two years. I began to wonder if I had done something to tick Maude off. If that was the case, no one had communicated it with me. There just didn't seem to be any logical reasoning behind the decisions being made.

With the possibility of obtaining an administrative job in the district seemingly miniscule, I realized I'd better start looking for another job right away.

* *

Many years ago when I started looking for a teaching job, I went to every school in which I was interested; whether they had an opening or not. I asked to see the principal, looked him or her in the eye, introduced myself, and shook hands. I know for a fact that making that extra effort earned me interviews for several of the teaching jobs I obtained. In today's educational job market that personal interaction is missing.

The vast majority of educational job opportunities are advertised on the Internet. There are several common websites that most districts use, and prospective employees are very familiar with these sites. Candidates apply online, upload their documents – cover letter, resume, transcripts, references, and letters of recommendation – and submit all of this information with a click of a button. There is no opportunity to make a personal impression on a possible employer.

Now, for a school district looking to hire someone, this system makes things much easier. Gone are the days of filing cabinets bursting with candidate files. Gone are the days of reading through stacks of printed resumes. Gone are the days of making a personal contact that opens the door for future employment.

Currently, districts will have several key people (principal, department head, etc.) go online, check the candidates' documents, and make a list of their top choices. There might be close to 100 hopeful candidates, but that list is narrowed down to about seven or eight people. There is no face-to-face involvement until the interviews take place. Speaking as someone who has been a part of the interview process as an employer, what you see on paper is not always what you get in person. I have been a part of several first round interviews that were painful, embarrassing, or so unbelievable that those of us involved struggled to keep a straight face.

In today's world of education, there are some unwritten rules when looking for a job. First, going to the school or district office and introducing yourself is frowned upon. Even emailing a prospective employer is discouraged. The only accepted thing a candidate can do to separate herself from the dozens of applicants is to have someone call on her behalf. Usually that person is the immediate supervisor.

It is unfortunate that the information that appears on a computer screen defines a person. Don't get me wrong – I love technology. It just seems that our transition to a paperless world is taking something away from the value of face-to-face interaction.

* *

Up until the day I found out I wouldn't be considered for the middle school position, I had never seriously considered the possibility that I would leave the school district. Naïve as it was, I still pictured myself finishing my career in the district in which I had worked for 14 years. Yes, they told me that if I remained in my current position there would be no guarantees. I guess in the back of my mind, I assumed something would come up for me. But you know what they say about assuming...

* *

For the first time in 14 years I was looking for a job. A feeling of sadness descended upon me. With a heavy heart, I bravely went to my filing cabinet to dig out my dusty resume. Of course I hadn't looked at it in over a dozen years. There had been no reason to update it – until now.

Having been out of the resume-writing business for so long, I asked a colleague of mine for some advice. She sent me an electronic copy of her current resume. As I looked it over, an overwhelming feeling rushed over me. I had 14 years of information to add to my resume. How would I ever remember the conferences I'd attended, the committees on which I had served, and all the leadership roles I had taken on? My Master's Degree information also needed to be added and my references updated. This task was going to take longer than I had initially anticipated.

After completing the daunting task of updating my resume, I logged on to the primary educational job search website used in my state. There was a five-page application that needed to be filled out. Most of the required information was the same as the contents of my resume. It was a time-consuming but relatively easy task. I had to go back to the filing cabinet to find my current teaching/administrative license to determine the exact names and numbers of my areas of certification. I also needed to locate my three sets of transcripts in order to provide my grade point averages and number of credits earned.

I uploaded all of this onto the site, as well as three letters of recommendation. (Back in May, when I realized I might need to start looking for a job sooner rather than later, I had asked several of my colleagues if they would write letters for me.) Finally, the task was complete. I was exhausted, but relieved.

With all my paperwork in order, I was now ready to look for any available positions as a school administrator.

* *

We live in an area of the state consisting of several medium-sized cities surrounded by smaller towns. Populations range from 66,000 to 73,000 people in the larger cities and 15,000 to 25,000 people in the smaller towns. Each city has its own school district; therefore, I had numerous options when applying for an administrative position relatively close to home.

In late June 2011, I found two elementary principal openings. One position was in the town adjacent to where we lived, the other was in a town just south of us. It would be a maximum 20-minute drive to work. I applied online for both jobs and uploaded all applicable paperwork.

One thing I had forgotten about was the cover letter. I obviously hadn't written a cover letter in 14 years, so it was back to the Internet to look for some help. Navigating through all the available sites to find exactly what I was looking for took quite a while. Most of these sites are geared toward the business world; however, I finally located a few samples that would work for me. I know you're supposed to personalize each cover letter to the specific employer and job situation, so I abided by this rule and personalized each cover letter. I read through the qualifications each district was looking for and tailored my letters as needed. I read each letter over at least twice to check for errors, and then submitted them online to the appropriate districts.

When I finally turned my computer off, I felt a great sense of accomplishment. I had spent hours gathering information and preparing my application materials. Most of the background work was done, so any future job applications would take less time. Over the course of the next few weeks, I waited for the phone to ring, however, I heard nothing. I didn't even get a "We regret to inform you..." email from either district. I figured with so many applicants, districts don't have the time (or don't take the time) to inform candidates that they have not been selected to interview. Still, it would have been nice to hear something.

5

JULY 2011
MORE JOB APPLICATIONS AND
MORE HEALTH ISSUES

Federal Unemployment Rate: 9.1%
Total Number of Jobs Applied For: 6
Total Number of Interviews: 0

In July I applied for four more administrative positions. Although I felt no sense of urgency, I expanded my search to include districts further away from where I was currently living. One position for a high school associate principal was in a city about 40 miles north and another was 40 miles to the west. If I were to land an interview at either of these places, it would be a good experience for me. I hadn't interviewed outside of my own school district for 14 years.

During this time I also checked into post-secondary positions. I had taught part-time for several years at Austin Community College, which gave me post-secondary experience. Although I had no administrative experience at that level, I thought I'd give it a shot. There was an opening at a college for a Job Placement Coordinator. This position involved working as the go-between person with school districts and the college to find placement for student teachers. I thought it would be perfect for me, so I applied. I didn't get an interview, but I did get an email saying "thanks but no thanks."

* *

By this time I had made a full recovery from my two surgeries; however, the pain in my groin had not gone away and the pain in my hip was getting progressively worse. I decided to see a second orthopedic surgeon.

This surgeon specialized in hip and knee replacements. He designed the replacement parts and was passionate about his work. When I met with him, he impressed me with his vast knowledge. I had several x-rays taken just before my appointment and as we looked them over, it became obvious to me why I was in so much pain. My right hip was bone on bone, which had made my right leg a bit shorter than my left. No wonder I had been limping for months.

The doctor told me that it was time to do a total hip replacement. Although I was still relatively young for the procedure, I agreed.

I found out that there was a process involved when preparing for a hip replacement. There were tests to be run, medicines to start taking, others to stop taking. Therefore, it would be at least a month before I could schedule my surgery. Recovery for a hip replacement is anywhere from eight to twelve weeks, depending on your job. Due to the amount of standing and walking I do in my job, my doctor recommended that I take at least 10 weeks off. I told him that I would need to discuss the timing of the surgery with my husband and my employer.

It was already too late in the summer to have the surgery before school started. If I did, it would mean missing the first five or six weeks of school, which is one of the busiest times of the year. That meant I would have to get it done once school started. After talking to Boyd, and then Debra, I scheduled my surgery for Wednesday, September 28.

Having my surgery at the end of September would allow me to be at school for the entire first month. Homecoming was scheduled for the weekend right before September 28, so I would be there to help out with that big event. I would be out until the week after Thanksgiving, allowing me almost nine weeks of recovery time – less than my doctor had advised.

Fortunately, I had not missed much school in the 14 years I had been in the district, allowing me to amass quite a few sick days. Even after using about three weeks worth of sick days in May, due to my two previous surgeries, I still had plenty of days left.

In reality, I was not that worried about missing two months of school. Remember, James was coming to the high school this year, giving us an extra associate principal, so I would not be leaving them high and dry. I knew that the other associate principals would be fine covering for me for two months.

Part of me wondered whether anyone - Maude, Troy, even Debra – thought I was having the surgery now in order to use up my sick days. Or maybe they thought I was doing it to get back at them for laying me off. I hoped that wasn't the case.

* *

During July, I was able to take some time off of work to relax and accomplish a few tasks around the house. There is no summer school during the week of the July 4 holiday and typically all the administrators take that week off. Each administrator is given either 20 or 25 vacation days each year, determined by how many years one has served in the district. Most of us found it difficult to use them all up because it was frowned upon to use them during the school year.

Due to the fact that I had several carry-over days from the previous school year, I had over 30 vacation days that I needed to use between July 1, 2011 and June 30, 2012. If I were truly leaving the district, I wanted to use up those vacation days. If I didn't use them, I would lose them. So I took a few days here and there during the summer, giving me several long weekends to enjoy.

6

AUGUST 2011
FAKING IT

Federal Unemployment Rate: 9.1%
Total Number of Jobs Applied For: 10
Total Number of Interviews: 0

With the school year quickly approaching, work started picking up for me. It was now August, and I continued checking the various educational job websites for openings.

As a school administrator on a 12-month contract, I was doing my entire job search outside of the workday; however, I found myself thinking about my situation all the time. Would it be possible to find a different job before the school year started? What if I find a job after staff and students return? What about my hip replacement surgery? Do I really want to find another job now? I loved my job so much; I really didn't want to leave it any sooner than I had to. Despite having received no interviews, I was still both hopeful and dreading having to be in the difficult situation of having to let my high school administrative team know that I would be leaving to take a new job.

With all that said, I applied for four more positions during August. Two of the positions were relatively close to home and two were quite a bit further away. Lexie, one of the administrative assistants at the high school, knew of my situation. She has a daughter who teaches in a school district about 100 miles south of us. I had actually taught her daughter when she was in middle school. So with a former student of mine putting in a good word for me, I applied for the opening – a middle school associate principal.

If I were to get the job, it would mean getting an apartment in the school district, living there during the week and returning home on the weekends. Not an ideal situation, but I thought I'd take a chance. As it turned out, I did not get an interview. I later found out that they had hired a person with a PhD – for an associate principal position! What? It didn't make sense to me, but not a whole lot was making sense at the time.

Another position I found that would mean living apart from Boyd during the week was a job in the business world. When no interviews were happening for me with school districts, I started looking online for jobs outside of education. With my background as a teacher, I considered taking a job with a company who provides training for employees or clients. I applied for an E-Learning Trainer position with a company who develops and installs medical software in hospitals. The ad for the job stated that applicants didn't need to have extensive knowledge of their product because they would train employees to become an expert. So I stepped away from my comfortable world of education and applied for the job.

A few days later I received an email from the company asking me to go online to complete a series of questions. These questions identified a person's personality traits, strengths, and weaknesses. I was very excited to complete this because it meant they were possibly considering me for an interview. Soon after I answered the online questions, disappointingly, I received an email stating I would not be considered for the position. Although I was stepping out of my comfort zone applying for a job outside of education, it was still a disappointment to not be selected for an interview. Quickly becoming discouraged, I outwardly remained hopeful that something would pop up; after all, I at least had a position for the next year.

* *

Our district-wide Administrative In-service takes place every August. For two days, all the central office and building administrators get together to prepare for the upcoming school year. The night before the in-service began, I asked God to help me get through the following two days. Normally, I enjoyed the time with my colleagues who had become friends; this year I was absolutely dreading it.

I feared seeing all the looks of pity from the other administrators. They all knew this would be my last year, but like me, no one knew why that decision had been made. So it was with much trepidation that I walked into the middle school library for the first day of our Administrative In-service.

My safety zone was obviously with the other high school associates, however, there was no room left at their table. Feeling awkward and conspicuous, I stood there looking around for a place to sit, certain that everyone was staring at me. I just wanted to sit down and disappear. Finally, to my relief, a central office administrator stood up from the high school table and offered me his chair. I sat down quickly and looked down, pretending to look for something in my purse.

Our first activity that opening day proved to be my undoing. We were each supposed to stand up, state our name, where we work, how long we'd been in the district, and tell everyone what we were most looking forward to this school year. If our table had gone first, maybe this activity wouldn't have been so hard for me. As it turned out, we were one of the last tables to share.

One by one, the administrators stood and shared the required information. I'm not usually nervous in situations like this, but for some reason, I was getting very anxious. While waiting for my turn, I tried to think of what I was most looking forward to this year. What I wanted to say was, "A guaranteed job for the following year." With that thought now ingrained in my mind, I felt my throat start to close. I tried to calm myself. I had to get through this without losing it emotionally.

Finally, it was my turn.

I stood up and, in a mostly steady voice, said, "I'm Nancy Chessman, associate principal at the high school. This will be my 15th year in the district." Until that last sentence I was fine. Had I skipped that sentence, I probably would have gotten through my spiel. However, when I spoke of my numerous years in the district, I started to choke up. My mind was screaming, "This is my 15th year in this district, damn it, and

I'm getting pushed out the door!" I tried so hard to keep it together, but my emotions, always so close to the surface these days, did not allow me to remain composed.

With a quivering voice, and tears welling in my eyes, I completed my turn, saying, "What I'm most looking forward to this year is continuing to build relationships with the staff and students at the high school." I hardly got the words out; it seemed to take forever to finish the sentence. As I spoke, I looked around the room. It was easy to see that most people felt uncomfortable. They all knew my situation and most were compassionate. As I scanned the room, a couple of my closest colleagues were nodding their heads, helping me get through my turn. I was so grateful for their support.

Sitting down and trying to compose myself, I don't think I said anything to anyone for quite awhile. I was embarrassed that I had choked up in front of everyone. It had evoked the looks I was dreading the most. I wish I could have been stronger instead of allowing everyone's pity to physically push in on me. At that moment, I would have given anything to be anywhere else but in that room. The problem with knowing a job is soon to end is that there is often this idea of "saving face" while having to still complete the job until termination is official.

For the remainder of the day, I found it very difficult to pull myself out of my awful mood. I tried to smile and interact with people, but there was such heaviness in my chest. The topics that were discussed that day went in and out of my head without retention. I couldn't concentrate on anything except my horrible situation. I was sad, felt sorry for myself, and I didn't care anymore who saw it.

At the end of the day, I left as quickly as possible, hardly saying goodbye to anyone. I needed to get away from everyone and try to forget about what had happened that morning. I hadn't been home more than ten minutes when my phone rang. It was Debra. She wanted to meet me for a drink at a nearby bar and grill. I really didn't want to go, but she was my immediate supervisor, and I felt obligated.

We sat at a table on the outdoor patio and each ordered a beer. Debra wanted me to know that she could relate to what I was going through. She told me of a somewhat similar situation she had gone through and gave me some ideas on how to get through the upcoming school year. I listened to what she had to say, and even though it didn't make me feel any better, I was grateful that she cared enough to offer advice.

I wondered if Maude had told Debra to meet with me. It had been apparent to everyone, during the long day, that I was not handling my situation well. There was still another day of in-service, and I could imagine Maude not wanting to deal with a depressed administrator in the group. On the other hand, Maude was so cold, she may not have even noticed my emotional struggle that day.

Thankfully, the next day was a bit easier. At one point I had to stand up and present some information our group had compiled. Since it had nothing to do with me personally, I was able to present without issue. It was the beginning of my journey through the upcoming school year in which I became an expert at plastering a fake smile on my face, hiding my true emotions, and pretending nothing was wrong.

7

SEPTEMBER 2011
THE BEGINNING OF THE END

Federal Unemployment Rate: 9.0%
Total Number of Jobs Applied For: 10
Total Number of Interviews: 0

The first day of school was my LAST first day of school at the high school, and most likely, in the school district. It was a bittersweet, emotional day. How great it was to see everyone again after summer break. Students were dressed in new clothes carefully picked out for the first day of school. Boys were sporting fresh haircuts exposing tan lines around their scalps. Girls screamed at the sight of friends they hadn't seen in weeks, or perhaps months, then proceeded with bear hugs.

I stood at my post in the hallway, observing the first day rituals with very mixed feelings. The start of every new school year brings with it the hope of success for all students. Some students will achieve beyond expectations: academically, athletically, or in some other capacity. Other students will struggle with their studies and/or their behavior. I had interactions with all of these students, and as I stood welcoming them back to school, I knew my daily influence on them was coming to an end.

Some of these students I had known for several years; some of their families I'd known for over a dozen years. I knew I had nine months left to work with these young adults, but after that, who knew what I would be doing? So it was with my real feelings hidden that I greeted them that day, smiling and laughing as if nothing in the world was wrong.

Troy, one of our assistant superintendents, had made it a practice to always show up at the high school on the first day of classes. He liked to connect with the administrators, staff, and students and wish everyone a successful school year. When he rounded the corner and walked toward me, I looked away. Every time I saw Troy or Maude, a feeling of anger welled up inside me. I did not know why I was being laid off, and I did not know whom to blame. All I knew was that in a very short amount of time, I would no longer have a job.

With Troy approaching me, I forced a smile and greeted him.

"Good morning Nancy! How are you doing today?" Troy asked, flashing a grin.

I knew he was just being polite, however, I wanted to reply, "How do you think I'm doing, Troy? This may be the last year I work in this district. I'm not doing well at all!"

Instead, averting my eyes, I replied, "Fine."

"It's nice to have the students back again for another year, isn't it?" he said, seemingly oblivious to my situation.

Another one-word reply from me, "Yes."

To my relief, he walked off. Anger once again welled up in me, and tears threatened to overspill my eyes. Troy was either unaware, or was ignoring, how devastated I was due to the situation he and Maude had put me in. He interacted with me as if nothing had changed.

I remained in the hallway until all the students made their way to their first hour class. Although my time to help these students was short, I decided that day that I was going to give them all I had for the upcoming school year; just as I had done for the past 29 years in which I had been an educator.

* *

With the start of a new school year came the start of football season. One responsibility of being a high school administrator was supervising all of the home football games. Even if our team was losing more than winning, there was always a crowd at the home games. For that reason, the whole administrative team was present for each game.

Being a former middle school teacher, I was assigned to supervise the middle school students that, without fail, came to the games. Let me make it clear up front; the middle school students did not come to watch the game. They came for three reasons: 1) to get away from their parents on a Friday night, 2) to goof around the whole time, oblivious of the score, and 3) to make the game supervisors' evening a living hell. Also, once the cold November nights arrived, there would still be a few boys in shorts and a few girls with spaghetti straps and no jacket. Sigh...

There was an area right next to the concession stand in which these middle school kids liked to hang out. The girls spent most of their time gossiping and flirting with the boys. The boys spent most of their time chasing each other around, throwing things, or trying to hit each other in the crotch.

Every once in awhile it was necessary for me to walk behind the concession stand - an off-limits area for the students. Most of the time it was clear, however, sometimes I'd run across two kids making out. It wasn't a pretty sight. I would break it up and we'd all be on our way.

It may sound like I did not enjoy supervising the football games, and there were a few freezing and/or rainy evenings in which I would have given anything to be home. Most of the time, though, it was fun. The atmosphere was always energized; families and community members packed the stands, the band performed at halftime, and the cheerleaders led the crowd in support of the team.

After every home game the administrative team, along with our spouses, went to Debra's house for a little down time. We would drink a few beers and eat pizza and chips. It was a great way to unwind after a busy week. At least that's how I looked at it during my first year at the high school. This year I felt differently.

Debra and Troy were very good friends, and she invited him to all the post-football game gatherings at her house. Troy is actually a lot of fun to hang out with, however, my relationship with him had become strained since he and Maude had given me the bad news last April. Due to this, I was not looking forward to going to Debra's house after the football games this year.

At our first post-game gathering, there was an excitement in the air. We had won the game and it looked as if our football team was headed for a winning season. With 10 people present, all gathered around the food in Debra's kitchen, it was a rowdy group.

"Who needs a drink?" Troy shouted.

"Toss me a beer!" Max replied.

Troy then turned to me and said, "What would you like, Nancy? A beer? A mixed drink?"

"Thanks, I'll have a beer," I responded.

As he handed me a cold beer from the refrigerator, I wondered, once again, if Troy was totally unaware of my state of mind. Didn't he notice that I was not actively involved in any of the conversations? Could he not see the raw emotion that I was barely hiding just under the surface?

As I stood on the periphery of all conversations, with a fake smile on my face, watching everyone interact animatedly, a different idea entered my mind. Maybe Troy was choosing to ignore my situation. To make himself feel better? To make me feel better? And, what could he possibly say to me anyway to improve my demeanor or to change my situation? Whatever the case, I felt uncomfortable and left the party after only a short time.

With my hip replacement surgery scheduled for the end of the month, I was only going to supervise three home football games. By the time I returned to school after Thanksgiving, the season would be over. I was actually relieved that I would only have to spend three evenings at Debra's house with Troy present. I could have skipped the gatherings all together, but I felt obligated to go. I didn't want to strain my relationship with Debra during my last year at the high school.

* *

Our city is relatively small with a population of approximately 25,500. A large lake borders the entire east side, which attracts boaters and fishermen throughout the year. The downtown area stretches for about a mile on the northeast edge of town. Small shops and restaurants line both sides of the street. A bank, the library, and our new medical center inhabit the largest buildings. Next to the library is a grassy area with a small stage that is used for summer lunchtime concerts and the Saturday Farmers Market.

For one weekend in June, our main street is closed to traffic. Numerous basketball hoops are set up on makeshift courts for a three-on-three basketball tournament. This event has been an annual tradition for years, each year drawing more and more players and spectators.

On the eastern end of our main thoroughfare is a park that borders the lake, complete with playground equipment for the kids and a pavilion equipped with a stage for summer events. Moored sailboats dot the water bordering the park creating a picturesque view. A fountain, complete with statues of children playing in the water, welcomes all who enter the park.

The city holds an annual July 4th Celebration at this park every summer, which is always well attended. There are food and game booths, inflatable bounce houses for the kids, and local entertainment on the stage. Folks spread blankets and tarps out on the water's edge, usually the day before, in order to save the best spot for viewing the fireworks.

During the Christmas season, lights adorn the trees that line the downtown area, decorations are hung on the streetlights, shops decorate their windows, and music plays on speakers for all to hear. Our downtown area is the best part of our city. The events that take place there are anticipated and well attended. One of these events is the high school Homecoming Parade.

Homecoming is one of the highlights of the year at the high school. Filled with preparations and anticipation, the week of Homecoming includes not only the requisite football game and dance, but also a Homecoming Parade.

At five o'clock on a chilly Friday afternoon in September 2011, about two hours before the start of the football game, the high school Homecoming Parade began. For several years, the building administrators from the school district had participated in the parade. The first year we walked the parade route. A couple of years later the elementary principals rode in a boat being towed by a truck. Being a competitive bunch, the high school administrators wanted to top that. Lexie, one of our administrative assistants, was able to obtain a vintage fire truck for us to ride on during the parade. We knew we had outdone the other principals! We bought giant bags of candy; enough, it seemed, to supply hundreds of kids with all the candy they wanted. We were all very excited about the opportunity to ride on the fire truck. Sadly, a voice kept whispering in my head, "This is your LAST Homecoming Parade."

When I arrived at the meeting spot, I spied the fire truck. It was a vintage model that would allow us all a spot to sit, high above the ground, in the back of the truck. Looking around as the floats were getting in the correct order, the band was warming up, and students were excitedly talking, I felt heaviness in my chest. I would never experience this again with this group of students and adults. My eyes started to well up with tears, and I walked quickly to a spot where no one could see me trying to compose myself. This was supposed to be a highlight of the school year. Instead, for me, I felt extreme sadness.

Once I pulled myself together, I walked toward the fire truck to meet up with the other high school administrators. I decided that I was going to enjoy the parade, so I did my best to push the current circumstances of my life to the back of my mind.

Soon, the band, accompanied by the flag squad and the cheerleaders, led the parade down the main drag, playing the school fight song. Floats, decorated by the students over the past month, carried athletic teams and various club members. Families lined the parade route, waiting to see their teenagers who were participating in the parade. Older folks sat in lawn chairs, having witnessed the parade for many years. Young children stood at the edge of the curb with their hands out, yelling, "Candy, here! Candy, here please!"

While riding on that fire truck, down the length of our main downtown street, I smiled and waved at many familiar faces, threw candy to the children, and really tried to enjoy myself. There were moments in which I was able to take pleasure in the experience, but most of the parade I was fighting tears. The rest of the administrative team riding on the fire truck was oblivious to what I was feeling.

I saw so many families whose children I had taught. The parents waved and called out to me. None of them knew that this was going to be my last year in the district. Many of these families had been a part of my daily interactions for years; I had taught most or all of their children. Yet this was the end. What a rollercoaster of emotions I experienced during that parade.

* *

After the parade, all the administrators headed back to the high school. The football game would be starting in a little over an hour and we needed to be on site to deal with any last minute issues. The other associate principals and I were able to grab a quick bite to eat in the alumni tent. It would be the last few minutes to relax before our supervising duties began.

In front of a large crowd, our football team won the game. By the end of the game my hip was really hurting. I'd been on my feet quite a bit that day - during school, at the parade, and at the football game. I was ready to just go home and sit down. That was not to be. For the last time that year, I was heading over to Debra's house for our post-game get-together. Boyd had decided not to attend this time, so I headed over on my own.

When I arrived, I knew I wasn't going to stay long. I hated the fact that this unexplainable situation kept ruining my mood and my ability to have fun. As much as I kept trying to put it out of my mind, it was always there. And knowing that Troy would be there to throw a few beers back and joke with the admin team did not help my state of mind.

In some ways I was upset with my colleagues for not being more intuitive, for not seeing how down I was feeling, but then I realized that they couldn't truly perceive the feelings I had hidden under a smiling, humor filled mask.

As was becoming the norm, I ended up having one beer and then leaving. I just wasn't in the mood to laugh or joke around. When I got home, Boyd could tell that I wasn't myself. He knew what was bothering me, but didn't bring it up. And for that I was grateful.

* *

On the morning of September 28, Boyd and I woke up at 4:00 a.m. I was supposed to be at the hospital at 5:30 a.m. to get checked in and situated in my hospital room. My doctor scheduled his surgeries on Mondays, Wednesdays, and Fridays. There were usually five or six scheduled each day. On each of his surgery days, the doctor would arrive at the hospital, look over the charts of his patients scheduled for that day and then decide in which order he would operate.

When Boyd and I arrived at the hospital that morning, I did not know whether I would be the first or last in the operating room. My surgery could begin at 7:00 a.m. or as late as 1:00 p.m. I was hoping to be first, but luck hadn't been on my side much lately, and I was not very optimistic.

At 6:20 several nurses scurried into my room, saying we needed to hurry because I was first on the operating schedule for the day. I was ecstatic – something was finally going my way. They started my IV, gave me the anti-nausea drug I had requested, as I have issues with vomiting after anesthesia, and wished me luck. The doctor popped in briefly to say hello and verify that it was my right hip being replaced. I then got a kiss from Boyd and was wheeled to the operating room.

Although this was major surgery, including sawing some of my bones and pounding metal objects into others, I hadn't been all that nervous about it. I had been in so much pain for so long that I couldn't wait to have a brand new hip.

As expected, the surgery went very well. When I woke up, I felt no pain because I had been filled with major pain-killing drugs. The nurses told me that I would be getting morphine shots on an as-needed basis. Since the medicine took a while to get into my system, they advised me, "Don't try to be brave. Keep the pain under control at all times. Hit your call button as soon as you start feeling even the slightest pain." I followed their instructions and received morphine shots at the first sign of pain. By late afternoon, although I was feeling very little pain in my hip, my head was throbbing.

I am a lightweight when it comes to medicine and drinking. I always take the least amount of medicine necessary, especially when it comes to painkillers. If I take too much, my stomach gets upset. When drinking, if I have more than one beer or alcoholic beverage, I'm tipsy. Yes, I'm a cheap date.

So when I complained to the nurses that my head felt like it was going to explode, they gave me a different kind of painkiller, in addition to the morphine, to hopefully get rid of my headache. By the middle of the night, my head was still pounding. Just turning my head on the pillow was a new experience in pain. When the nurse came in for my vitals check – inevitably just after I had fallen asleep – I let her know about my persistent headache. She figured that the morphine shots were causing the headache and decided to put an order in for me to take the morphine orally. Hopefully, taken in a different form, the morphine would not cause my headache to continue.

The following morning I was given two morphine pills. Within a couple of hours, my headache had weakened a bit. My head still hurt, but at least I could move it around without the pain I had suffered the day before.

At 9:00 a.m. the physical therapist came for her first visit - only 24 hours after my surgery. Today's lesson was learning how to get in and out of bed. After a hip replacement, I had to be very careful regarding how I moved. There was always a chance of popping out the new hip. If that happened, it would mean taking the brand new hip out and getting a totally new replacement.

So with that fear deeply instilled in me, I received my first lesson on how to move around safely. Carefully, the physical therapist helped me maneuver myself to a sitting position on the edge of the bed with my feet on the floor. She then put a harness around my waist in case I slipped. Using a walker for leverage I stood up. Surprisingly, it was relatively easy and there was no pain. I took a few slow, small steps forward and then backward before I sat back down on the bed. We repeated this procedure one more time before I was told that was it for the day.

My headache never totally went away that day, but it was manageable, so I continued to take morphine pills orally. I had several family members visit, including Boyd, which helped pass the time. When I was alone, I read, watched TV, or slept.

The following day I took a walk down the hall using the walker for support. I walked farther than even I expected, and it felt great. My physical therapist taught me not only how to walk correctly with a walker but also how to turn around. Any wrong move could dislocate the new hip, and I was paying close attention to all her instructions.

At the end of my session the physical therapist said, " You're doing so well! You're my star patient."

"The only reason for that is because all of your other patients are in their 80s!" I replied.

I was taken off of morphine that day and put on a different pain pill. As soon as I stopped ingesting morphine, my headache went away. It was such a relief having that two-day headache finally gone. After work, when Boyd visited me, I went for another walk, mainly to show him all the progress I was making.

On Saturday, my release day, I had one more session with the physical therapist. This lesson was how to walk up and down stairs using a handrail and my collapsed walker. I was told I could only climb two or three stairs – enough to get in and out of the house. Since we lived in a two-story house, I would not be able to go upstairs for a month. Knowing this ahead of time, we had set up Kayla's childhood twin bed in the living room at home.

As I left the hospital, the physical therapist walked out to the car with Boyd and me. She had one last lesson – how to get in and out of a car. It was amazing to me how we take for granted all our movements throughout the day. Getting in the car with a new hip replacement, although not painful, was a process. I was not to bring my knee up toward my chest; that's the position that will dislocate the hip. Out of all the movements I would make over the next few months, I was most careful while getting in and out of the car.

We arrived home safely; Boyd helped me into the house and onto the bed in the living room. And with that I began my two months of recovery time.

8

OCTOBER 2011
REST, RECOVERY,
AND A LUCKY BREAK

Federal Unemployment Rate: 8.9%
Total Number of Jobs Applied For: 10
Total Number of Interviews: 0

Until the last week, October was a quiet month. I spent the majority of my time either propped up or lying down in bed. Following doctor's orders, I rested, letting my new titanium hip adhere to my bones.

Boyd was home with me the first few days: fixing meals, bringing me needed items, and keeping me company. Surprisingly, I was able to get around with ease. I had mastered the art of getting in and out of bed, and with every day that passed, I felt more comfortable walking around the house.

About a week after my return home I was able to wean myself off of pain pills. After watching Boyd go through his knee replacement and recovery a few years prior, I thought I'd be on pain pills for much longer. I quickly realized that hip replacement surgery is a lot less invasive than a knee replacement. I was glad to be off the painkillers, especially since I'm such a lightweight.

In preparation for my surgery we had purchased a basket that attaches to the walker. Due to Boyd's knee replacement we already had a walker. So I was able to transport items – food, books, clothes – which made my life a bit more convenient when I was home alone.

When my family and friends visited, I repeatedly heard comments like, "Nice walker, old lady!" or "Hey, can I borrow that basket when you're done with it?" Everyone thinks they're a comedian!

My doctor had released me from the hospital with several exercises I was to do several times each day. Most of them involved tightening and stretching the muscles in my right leg. I was also supposed to take short, frequent walks. That was easy since I made many trips to the bathroom and the kitchen throughout the day.

Bathing was interesting during my first month home. We only have a half bath on our first floor. Even if we would have had a full bathroom, I was only allowed to take a shower if it was a walk-in shower stall. So that meant sponge baths for a month. Let's be honest, a damp washcloth with a little bit of soap only goes so far in cleaning the human body. All of that walking from the bathroom to the kitchen with a basket in tow really caused me to break a sweat, and the sponge bath just wasn't cutting it. To make matters worse, Kayla came home from college about 10 days after my surgery. The first thing she said upon entering the house was, "It smells like old people in here." I hoped it was the bed linens and not me that was producing the odor. Needless to say, the sheets went into the washing machine immediately, and I had Kayla spray Febreeze on all the furniture and carpets.

* *

During the first couple of weeks of my recuperation, I tried to distract myself with the exercises my doctor had assigned, TV, and puzzle books. It worked to an extent, however, my job situation was always lurking just below my conscious thoughts. A nagging voice inside my head kept saying, "You are going to be out of a job in just a few short months," and, "Now would be a really good time to apply for a job."

I checked the employment website, reluctantly, once a week, but there were no administrative openings anywhere in the area. The school year had been in session for over a month, and all open positions had already been filled.

* *

For over ten years I have been in a monthly book club with four other women. When we started the club we were all teaching at the same middle school. There were two English teachers, a science teacher, a Family and Consumer Education teacher (Home Economics for you old-timers like me), and myself, a math teacher. We lost the science teacher after a couple of years – she moved to Florida. Within two months we added another English teacher, so we were back to a group of five. Currently, we're almost all at different schools, which makes getting together once a month even more enjoyable.

Our book club is probably different than most. We do read a book each month; however, when we get together we spend very little time discussing it. Our gatherings last anywhere from two to three hours, and we discuss the book for maybe 10 minutes. The majority of our time is spent catching up on what has been happening with each of us over the past month. In other words, it's a good excuse to get away from husbands and kids, have a glass of wine or beer, and spend time with close friends.

Why read the book at all? First, it gives us an opportunity to read books we might not otherwise read. Second, we have the tradition of rating each book on a scale of one to ten. Usually a book will rate anywhere from seven to ten. Only on one or two occasions has a book been rated a five or below. Since we've read over 120 books, that's not too bad.

We have a rotating system for choosing the book and the place to meet. Typically we go to a restaurant, but not always. Sometimes the hostess will have book club at her house, out on the patio during the summer or indoors by the Christmas tree in December. One or two months we met at a movie theater to watch the movie version of a book we had read. Another time we had a woman who does make-your-own necklaces meet with us and we each made a necklace for ourselves. It was great fun and the necklaces revealed quite a bit about our individual tastes and personalities.

Our book club has also done some traveling. On two occasions we've driven a few hours north to spend a few days in a summer cabin. We played games, fished off the dock, did some shopping in town, and relaxed. Another year, after we'd read several books about the Amish, we traveled to Shipshewana, Indiana to visit an Amish museum and to hopefully spot some Amish people. We saw men driving horse-drawn buggies and women hanging typical, modest Amish clothing out to dry on clotheslines. While in town we visited several Amish-owned stores and bought some food items to take home.

Every December since its inception, our book club has done an ornament exchange. We try to find "original" ornaments with a $10-$15 spending limit. We all look forward to this tradition each year. Every time I decorate our Christmas tree, I remember which ornaments I've received from my book club friends – many of which are my favorites.

Although it was not my turn to pick the book for the month of October, I requested that we meet at my house. Since I was still using a walker, and not able to drive, I didn't want to burden one of my friends to pick me up. Additionally, I really didn't want to go out in public using a walker – that damn pride thing again. So, book club was held at my house this month. Everyone brought food, and I provided the drinks. It was so nice to have visitors – especially since these were my closest friends. It broke up my monotonous daily routine, even if for only a few hours.

It wasn't until after my girlfriends left that I realized how grateful I was for book club that month. I could have cancelled, using my hip replacement recovery as an excuse, but I was so glad I hadn't done that. These women were all aware of my situation and were truly concerned about me. I was trying to heal physically, while at the same time stay sane mentally. This was a group of women in which I could share any-thing, without judgement. They were an important part of my support system, and I appreciated their concern and their encouragement.

* *

We are a tennis family. As I mentioned earlier, Boyd and I played tennis on our first date. That became a regular activity throughout our courtship and then our marriage. Due to our love of the game, we wanted to pass it on to Kayla. By the time she was five years old, Boyd had Kayla out on a tennis court.

Throughout his teaching career, Boyd did quite a bit of coaching - football, basketball, track, tennis, and golf. He developed the ability to pick out technique flaws in an athlete after observing for only a few minutes. He worked with Kayla and me on our tennis games for many years.

We had a family membership at a local tennis club. Boyd and I played in several leagues, and Kayla took lessons. By the time Kayla began high school she was an accomplished player. Playing doubles on the Varsity tennis team all four years, she also made it to the State Tennis Tournament each year. During her senior year, she and her doubles partner placed third in the state meet. It was quite an achievement, and we were extremely proud of her.

In August of 2011 Boyd came home after playing tennis with a friend, complaining that he didn't feel well. As he rested on the couch he explained, "While I was playing during the second set, I felt like I couldn't catch my breath. The guys told me to sit down and take a break."

Worry filled me. "Were you able to play after that?" I asked.

"Well, I was also having chest pains, but they went away quickly," he replied.

I was glad Boyd had confided in me. We were both concerned; I told him to stay on top of this issue. About a week later, the same thing happened again. At that point we decided he should see his doctor.

After hearing Boyd's symptoms, the doctor ordered a stress test and an electrocardiogram in order to measure his heart activity. Both tests came back showing no abnormalities. Much to our dismay, Boyd experienced the same symptoms a few weeks later while playing in his tennis league. Once again, Boyd called his doctor for a follow up. This time the doctor ordered a myocardiogram, which records the movements of the heart. Nothing out of the ordinary was found.

In the following weeks, Boyd's symptoms continued. He was now experiencing chest pain and shortness of breath when he walked up a flight of stairs. He called his doctor to get some advice. Having ruled out any heart issues with a series of tests, the doctor prescribed an inhaler. His thought was that Boyd had developed asthma.

Several more weeks passed and the inhaler was not helping. We were becoming extremely concerned. Certainly, the fact Boyd's mother had died of a heart attack at the young age of 51 was forefront in our minds. She had been a heavy smoker most of her adult life, and cigarettes were a major cause of her death. Boyd was in his late 50s and, although he never smoked, he began to wonder if the continued symptoms were a warning about his heart.

So back to the doctor he went – for the third time. It was now mid-October. Boyd's doctor recommended a cardiologist, and an appointment was made for the following week. Due to the seriousness of the situation, I went with Boyd to his appointment. Having recently graduated from the walker to a cane, I felt a whole lot less conspicuous and was more comfortable going out in public.

The cardiologist looked over all the tests Boyd had taken in the months prior. He asked Boyd several questions about symptoms and family history. He then told us that in some cases stress tests, EKGs, and myocardial grams could show false negatives. We couldn't believe that three different tests could be wrong.

Due to Boyd's family history of heart disease, the cardiologist told us that the only way to rule it out would be to do a heart catheterization. This would involve running a catheter from the femoral artery in the groin all the way up to the heart. A dye would be injected to determine which, if any, arteries were blocked. If any blockage were found, a stent would be placed in the artery to keep it open for blood flow.

"I would recommend that the heart catheterization happen sooner rather than later," the cardiologist advised.

"Could this be done tomorrow?" I asked. I was very worried and didn't want to wait any longer for both of us to finally get some answers.

Boyd was a bit resistant, however, it was two against one, and so the procedure was scheduled for the following day.

Later, Boyd would thank me.

Very early the next morning, Boyd and I drove to the hospital. As we waited for the procedure, we marveled at the frequency of doctor's appointments, surgeries, and procedures we'd had over the past six months. This had not been a good year for us when it came to our health. I can't help but wonder how much the stress of looming unemployment was responsible for every malfunction within our bodies.

Soon Boyd was taken for his procedure. I would wait in the lounge until the doctor came with word on what was found in Boyd's heart. If there were a need for a stent, the doctor would let me know before proceeding. As I waited, I said numerous prayers. It seemed like forever before the doctor came to bring me the news, and I contemplated whether that was a good thing or a bad thing. The doctor finally arrived.

He informed me, "The main artery to Boyd's heart is 99% blocked. I will be putting in a stent in order to open the artery back up and allow blood to flow into the heart."

I was shocked, although the more I thought about it the more it made sense. Boyd had been having episodes for months, and with a family history of heart problems, he was at a higher risk.

Once Boyd was settled in a room, I was allowed to visit with him. When the doctor came by he told us, "If Boyd would have had even one more episode, he might have died." We found out that the artery that had been blocked is called "the widow maker."

Boyd was a lucky man.

After the doctor left, Boyd shared some details with me.

"Nancy, I was awake throughout the procedure. It was the worst thing I have ever gone through in my entire life. It felt like I was having a heart attack throughout the whole process. The pain was so unbearable, I thought I was dying."

I thought back to my three surgeries that year and said a silent prayer of thanks that everything had gone well. I also said a prayer thanking God for Boyd's successful procedure. I could have lost him and that scared me to the core. God had given him a second chance; he knew I would need Boyd's support as I dealt with the upcoming possibility of unemployment.

This health scare of Boyd's was the only thing that actually took my mind completely off of my job situation. While unemployment is certainly a huge cross to bear, when faced with the death of a loved one, we are given the opportunity of perspective. Boyd's close call made me realize that it's the people in our lives that really matter. A job can be replaced, a loved one cannot.

9

NOVEMBER 2011
LIBERATION

Federal Unemployment Rate: 8.7%
Total Number of Jobs Applied For: 10
Total Number of Interviews: 0

With the start of November came several milestones in my hip replacement recovery. Since I was now using a cane, I felt stronger, more stable when I walked, and more mobile. My daily walks now took me to the end of our long block and back. Although I had to wear a jacket, the temperatures remained warmer than usual.

Since I'd reached the one-month mark, I was able to go up a whole flight of stairs. That meant two things: I could sleep in my own bed, and I could take a shower. I cannot tell you how great that first shower felt. After a month of sponge baths, I finally felt totally clean. I was able to wash my hair without bending over the kitchen sink and shaving my legs became much less of a chore.

By mid-November I was cleared to drive again. That meant I was able to go grocery shopping and run other errands. I actually liked grocery shopping. That's a good thing because, when I sent Boyd, he would come back with numerous items that weren't on my list. These items usually involved sugary or salty snacks.

Due to these liberating changes, I was in a good mood most of the time. It had been awhile since that had occurred. Rarely did my job situation even enter my mind. Being away from school for so long had definitely improved my frame of mind. I was no longer dwelling on all the negatives and the "last" experiences at school.

Another reason for my good mood was the fact that the holidays were approaching. I loved decorating the house and spending time with family. Now that I was getting around more easily, I would be able to fully enjoy the holidays – with some help from Boyd and Kayla.

This year, it was my turn to host Thanksgiving for my family. Although I was still recovering from my hip surgery, I insisted on taking my turn. Boyd and Kayla would be around to help, and I thoroughly enjoyed hosting the event. Most of my family would be coming over to eat and watch football. It was always a fun day.

Regretfully, as Thanksgiving approached, so did my return to school. With mounting dread, I began counting down the days. Certainly I was excited to see everyone again – my administrative colleagues, the teachers, and the students, yet I knew that once I got back into the swing of things, all those depressing feelings would return.

On the Monday following Thanksgiving, I started back to work. I received many hugs and "welcome back" wishes, which reminded me how much my colleagues appreciated me. The warm welcome made my transition back quite a bit easier.

Soon it was as if I hadn't been gone at all. The only difference was that I could walk the halls with no pain and no limp. Going through major surgery and missing two months of school was worth the result. I felt great – at least physically. Mentally, well that was another matter altogether.

10

DECEMBER 2011
ANOTHER BOMBSHELL

Federal Unemployment Rate: 8.5%
Total Number of Jobs Applied For: 10
Total Number of Interviews: 0

December is a busy month for school administrators. With all the band, orchestra, and choir concerts, evening commitments increased during this time. Although it was time away from home, I thoroughly enjoyed the opportunity to observe the students in a different light. They were proud of their performance and appreciated when teachers and administrators were in attendance.

Our school has a large auditorium that includes a balcony. It seats almost 2,000 people. Not only does our school district use the auditorium, but different community groups also utilize the facility. It is used almost daily during the month of December.

Being the administrator on duty for a concert, I had several responsibilities. First, I am there to act as a resource person and problem-solver. I remember one concert in which the choir director forgot to reserve the first few rows of seats in the auditorium for the students participating in the show. Eager parents, family members, and students filled these seats. When the director realized her mistake, she had a mild meltdown. She asked me to make the uncomfortable announcement, asking all the people in the front three rows to move.

So up I went onto the stage, ready to be the bearer of bad news. I checked to make sure the microphone was on, and then informed the audience of the error. As I was speaking, I noticed how full the auditorium had already become. In order to allow the displaced people a place to sit, relatively close to the stage, I asked the rest of the audience to please move to the middle, filling in any empty seats. In an effort to lighten the mood, I said, "Pretend you're in church and slide to the middle please!"

To my delight, I got a few laughs!

Another responsibility of the administrator on duty is to be present in case of an emergency. During my first year at the high school, I chaperoned a band concert, along with a couple other administrators. Typically only one of us was required to be in attendance at a performance; however, the Marching Band Concert drew a big crowd, so we made sure there was adequate administrative presence.

The band director always did a fabulous job of making this a BIG event. Not only did the marching band members perform, but he also involved the cheerleaders, the flag team, and other people demonstrating school spirit. In an effort to top last year's show, the director had set up small platforms in the audience in which several members of the flag team would stand, performing their routine (audience participation was always a big part of this concert). As I watched the girls spinning and waving their flags, I had a premonition: "I'm glad I'm not sitting close to those spinning flags."

My bad feeling came to fruition. A woman in the audience was either sitting too close, or the flag girl spun her flag a bit too much in front of her. The woman was bonked in the head with the flagpole. Luckily we were there to call an ambulance.

The third, and probably most nerve-wracking, responsibility we have is to go up on stage before each event to welcome the crowd and to introduce the show. Each time it was my turn to introduce the show nerves would creep into my stomach, telling me that I would somehow embarrass myself. I would rehearse my short address over and over in my head until I felt confident. While most people think that administrators are comfortable in a leadership role, I know that even without my looming unemployment and the self-doubt the district had instilled in me, I still would have needed to breathe deeply before taking the stage.

* *

In mid-December, it was my turn to supervise the Holiday Choir Concert. On this particular December evening, just before walking onto the stage, I was feeling not only nervous, but also sad. This would be the last Christmas concert I would introduce and attend at the high school. Throughout the show, I sat in the auditorium and tried to forget about my situation and just enjoy the music.

They say music is a powerful thing, and in my case that is definitely true. There are certain songs that make me laugh, or get up and dance, and some that make me cry. On that evening, the final song sung by all the choirs was a moving rendition of Handel's Messiah. It brought tears to my eyes – for more reasons than just the beauty of this classic Christmas song. I struggled to not break down, knowing that in a few minutes I would be in the lobby greeting parents and students. It seemed as if my emotions were close to the surface more and more as the school year progressed.

* *

Soon after that concert I had a visit from Troy. I had no idea why he would be coming to see me in my office. He closed the door and sat in one of the uncomfortable chairs, usually reserved for students, across from my desk.

Not wasting any time with pleasantries, he said, "In the next couple of days some information is going to be presented to the administrators regarding changes in the district's retirement plans for all employees. Because Boyd works in the district, I want to make sure you understand that you cannot share any of the information with him."

"Of course not," I replied. "I can assure you that I will keep the information confidential."

I wondered why he was even telling me this. My questioning eyes met his. Then he said something that hit me so hard it felt as if I'd been shot in the chest.

"Maude is upset with you because you shared the news regarding James moving from the middle school to the high school with Boyd."

What? That had happened last spring - over seven months ago. Why was this being brought to my attention now? And how did they know that I had told Boyd? Troy advised me to speak with Maude about the situation right away.

As soon as he left the office, I called and made an appointment to see Maude. I did not tell Boyd about this – he was already so upset about my situation, and I didn't want to worry him any more than necessary. The next couple of days were grueling. I was totally stressed out, dreading the meeting.

When I finally met with Maude, I came with questions. She greeted me with a stone face. I sat down at the conference table, the same spot in which I had sat eight months ago to receive the life-changing news.

"I can't trust you anymore," she said, looking at me with eyes as cold as ice. "At the administrators' meeting last May, you were told to keep the information about James moving to the high school confidential. You told Boyd about it before James had a chance to inform his staff."

"Maude, I told Boyd the information because it directly affected me and my situation. I was going through a very difficult time, and I needed to confide in my spouse. I knew he wouldn't share the news with anyone, otherwise I wouldn't have told him."

I followed that by asking, "How did you even know that I had told Boyd?"

"Did you know that Boyd came to meet with me the day after the administrators were given the news about James?" She looked at me as if I was a mouse she had just caught in a trap.

"No," I responded, shocked. "He came to meet with you?"

"Yes," she said, her eyes never leaving mine. "He asked to meet with me, something I typically don't do. He spoke very highly of you and the job you are doing. He wanted me to know how committed you were to the students in our school district. During our conversation he made mention of James' move to the high school. That's how I found out you had not kept the news confidential."

I couldn't believe this was happening. Boyd went to speak to Maude with the best of intentions, but ended up only causing me trouble.

I reiterated to her that the only reason I had said anything to Boyd was because it was so closely tied to my situation, and I knew I could trust him not to say anything.

Looking at me with her steely eyes, she said, "None of that matters. You shouldn't have said anything."

"I'm sorry I didn't keep the news confidential," I said, feeling about as small as a fly on the wall. "I want you to know that you can trust me with information from this point on." She looked at me with doubt.

"Throughout the years in which I've been an administrator there have been dozens of things I've been privy to and have not shared with Boyd. The only reason I told Boyd about this particular topic was because I was personally involved." I was trying to plead my case, but the look on her face told me I was wasting my time. The thought once again entered my mind, "What had I done that made her turn against me in such a profound manner?"

I then asked her, "Why did it take over seven months for me to be informed you were upset? If you had an issue with me, I would rather have cleared it up right away."

"It is being addressed now because of the upcoming confidential information about retirement. I want to make sure you don't tell anyone, including Boyd."

That really did not answer my question. My thought was that she had obtained this tidbit of information about me and had saved it to use when she felt the time was right.

After apologizing again, or perhaps groveling, I asked if I would still be considered for a position within the district – administrative or teaching – for the following year.

"Let's say we have started the mending process." That was all she would commit to.

* *

Fortunately, a few days after that meeting, our winter recess began. I had never been more ready to take a break from work. I needed some time to forget about my job situation and looked forward to enjoying the holidays with my family. Kayla came home from college for a few weeks, which always put me in a good mood. The three of us were able to involve ourselves in all the Christmas traditions we had developed over the years. For a few days I was able to really enjoy myself without thinking about my job.

The house was already decorated for the holiday, complete with a Christmas tree in the living room, a large nativity scene on the mantle of the fireplace, and twinkling white lights on the bushes in front of the house. I had wound garland around the handrails by the stairs and had strategically placed several poinsettias around the house. We had done most of this decorating the weekend after Thanksgiving. I love the holidays and having the house all spruced up puts me in a good mood.

One evening, shortly after Kayla had arrived, we made Christmas cookies. This is a tradition started by my mom when my brothers and I were children. I now carry on the tradition with my family, using the same cookie and frosting recipe.

Kayla and I each have our respective roles in the cookie baking process. We have been doing this since she was old enough to use a cookie cutter, and, over the years, we developed a routine that works well for us. While I'm setting up our workspace, Kayla pops in a Christmas CD (usually Mannheim Steamroller). Then she pulls out our "cookie baking aprons." My apron is green with yellow trim. It's old - I bought it when I was pregnant with Kayla; however, I only wear it a few times a year, so it's still in really good condition.

Kayla's apron used to be mine when I was a child. My grandma made it for me – talk about traditions. The fabric is pink gingham with rick a rack trim. The apron is supposed to be tied around the waist, however, in order to keep flour off her shirt, Kayla ties it around her chest. It's hilarious; just another tradition she started years ago that has to be followed!

With aprons in place, music playing, and the oven preheating, I roll out the homemade cookie dough to the correct thickness. Kayla then uses the cookie cutters to form Christmas trees, stockings, snowmen, stars, and bells. Using a spatula, I place the cutout cookies on a baking stone. Because my hands are covered in flour and cookie dough, Kayla is in charge of placing the cookies in the oven, taking them out when they're done, and placing them on waxed paper on the countertop. We have the process down to a science, so we are able to talk, share, sing and laugh throughout the task.

After the cookies are cooled, we frost and decorate them. Boyd likes to join in this task because he can sample his work! I mix up the frosting while Boyd and Kayla set out the decorations – colored sugars, chocolate jimmies, and red hots. Boyd thinks every cookie should be decorated with at least five red hots. Each year Kayla and I have to remind him to limit the number he puts on the cookies! Another annual tradition.

Despite everything going on with my employment, life has a way of providing respite.

* *

Christmas Eve is when my immediate family celebrates the holiday. During the day we play board games and card games. While I'm preparing dinner, Boyd and Kayla always play Ping-Pong. Their laughter and shouts of a successful slam fill the house.

Every year, without fail, before dinner, Kayla asks, "Can we open gifts before we eat?" Every year we say, "No!"

That Christmas Eve, as always, there were plenty of gifts. Kayla and I received clothes, shoes, and jewelry. Boyd received an electronic reader, complete with a cover and a gift card to purchase several books.

After presents are opened and the mess is cleaned up comes our last Christmas Eve tradition – watching the Ron Howard/Jim Carrey version of *How the Grinch Stole Christmas*. While Kayla sets up the DVD, Boyd makes grasshopper drinks in the blender. After the movie, we head off to bed.

Christmas Day is spent at my mom's house with the rest of my family. I have three younger brothers, each married with children, so mom's house is full. There is an abundance of laughter, presents, games, and good food. As always, the day is over too quickly.

Over the winter break, I decided to go online to check for job openings. It had been a couple of months since I had checked the websites, and with some time off work I thought I'd take a chance. With a new semester approaching I thought something might be available. Unfortunately, there were no job openings in our area. But it was early; I still had months and months to find a new position. So I relaxed and enjoyed the remainder of my time off.

11

JANUARY 2012
PHASED OUT

Federal Unemployment Rate: 8.3%
Total Number of Jobs Applied For: 10
Total Number of Interviews: 0

D ebra, my immediate supervisor, had been told of my decision to stay at the high school in April of 2011. At that point, she made some changes in my responsibilities for the 2011-12 school year. One change involved which teachers I would supervise and evaluate. Due to the fact that I had such a strong math background, I had always worked with, and evaluated, the teachers in the math department. The math department at the high school consisted of about 15 teachers. During the 2010-11 school year I had also supervised the science department, which consisted of about 15 teachers.

Supervising and evaluating teachers involves several things. In the fall, administrators meet with the teachers to discuss their goals for the year. Throughout the school year, the administrator visits the teachers' class-rooms, formally and informally. These visits can be short (5 to 10 minutes) or long (the entire 45 minute class). This gives us a good idea of what is going on in each classroom, academically and socially. Administrators also meet with and assist these teachers as needed during the year. We attend their department meetings on occasion and are their go-to person for questions and needs. Toward the end of the school year, the administrator writes a formal assessment on the teachers' performance. We meet, once again, to discuss the evaluation and progress made on their goals.

During the summer of 2011, when our administrative team met to discuss teacher supervision responsibilities, I received a big surprise. I no longer was responsible for the math and science departments. I was given the health and music teachers to evaluate. Now, there is nothing wrong with supervising the health and music teachers. I actually loved going into those classrooms. I purposefully visited the music classrooms when I needed to escape from the piles of work in my office. Listening to the music – whether in voice or instruments – calmed me and put me in a good mood.

Walking into a health classroom was always interesting. You never knew what to expect. One day I walked into a health class to find a picture of a giant penis projected on the screen (human sexuality unit). Another time I walked in on four convicted drunk drivers, doing community service, telling their stories to the students.

My surprise at the change in my supervision responsibilities had little to do with the people or the subject matter – although I was disappointed that the math department was being taken away from me. My shock came in the form of numbers. I had always supervised 30 to 35 teachers. Now it would only be five teachers.

Although it would mean less work for me, I was very disappointed. I had formed a real connection with the math and science teachers in my first year at the high school. I couldn't believe that was being taken away from me. That's how I perceived the change – as a loss.

Another change that was made involved student management. For years, two of the Associate Principals at the high school dealt with student discipline. Each of the two administrators took two grades, splitting the load evenly. I found out during the administrative team meeting that there would now be three administrators dealing with student management. I would be responsible for two grades and each of the other two administrators would have one grade.

At that moment, the change didn't bother me. I enjoyed working with students to help them improve their behavior. The fact that I would have half of the student population was alright with me.

Later, when I was in my office looking over the assigned administrative responsibilities, it hit me. Many of the most important tasks an administrator performs were being taken away from me. I lost the majority of my teacher supervision tasks and had been given the greatest portion of student discipline. A light bulb went on in my head: I was being phased out.

I shared this information with Boyd when I got home that day, and he agreed with me. Because I had decided to stay on at the high school, they had to figure out what to do with me. Knowing I would be there for only one more year, I was given responsibilities that could easily be taken over by the other administrators the following year. Although I'm sure Debra did not change my responsibilities to hurt me; she had to think about the future good of the high school.

Another possibility was that Maude had spoken with Debra regarding my responsibilities. I wouldn't put it past her. Maude's hand was always into things and it certainly seemed that she had it in for me. I was still trying to figure out what I had done to her that resulted in my upcoming lay off. Whatever the reason for the administrative duty changes, it made me feel as if I'd been kicked a bit further out the door.

Teacher supervision and student management were only two of the responsibilities that changed for me that year. Some of the programs and events that had been in my charge were distributed to the other administrators. Summer School and Driver's Education had been my responsibility the previous year. This involved recruiting and hiring teachers, setting up student registration, keeping track of enrollment to determine whether the classes would run, among other things.

In January 2012, I began to receive phone calls from parents asking about summer school. Each time I directed them to the new administrator in charge, I felt sick. I never told the parents why a different administrator was running summer school, but I knew the reason. I would not be at the high school for the duration of Summer School. Someone else would be sitting in my office by that time.

From that point on, the reality of my situation began to take hold. A clock inside my head started ticking, drawing me closer and closer to the end of my days at the high school. And, the end of my days in the school district in which I had worked for almost 15 years. My stress level increased with every day that passed – not only because I would soon be without a job, but also because I would be forced to leave the school, staff, and students with whom I had grown very close.

12

FEBRUARY 2012
DODGING QUESTIONS

Federal Unemployment Rate: 8.3%
Total Number of Jobs Applied For: 10
Total Number of Interviews: 0

While the stress of my looming unemployment continued to build, life outside of work was also adding to my stress. I'm sure this is typical for anyone in an unemployment situation. Life's challenging circumstances, that might not otherwise be overwhelming, become even greater when added to an already high stress level.

Until this month, my mother lived in the home in which my brothers and I had grown up. Even after my dad died, she was healthy enough to live by herself. Over the past couple of years my mother's health had begun to deteriorate. She had been hospitalized several times and had taken a few nasty falls. Luckily she hadn't broken any bones yet, however, my brothers and I were getting worried.

We addressed our concerns with mom throughout the fall, but at that time she was not ready to move into an assisted living facility. After she had a couple of incidents occur within a short period of time, she let us make some inquiries. My brothers and I accompanied mom to several facilities and found one that she really liked.

On February 1, we moved mom into a two-bedroom apartment in an upscale assisted living community. We all felt relieved that mom would have people checking on her several times a day. She would have her meals prepared for her and would be with other people her age. There were daily activities in which she could participate, and she would still be free to drive herself to appointments and her weekly bridge games.

Moving mom from a three-bedroom home with a basement into an apartment meant leaving a lot behind. She was in no rush to sell her house, so mom and I decided that on Saturdays we would head over to her house and, room by room, go through everything. I really looked forward to those Saturdays. I knew that I was helping mom with a huge project that she couldn't do by herself. It also provided us with some valuable bonding time - and an opportunity for me to forget about my job situation for a while.

I would pick mom up about 9:00 in the morning, and we would work at her house for several hours. Systematically making our way through the house, I filled garbage bags and boxes with over 50 years of items that mom had acquired.

After mom and I had worked for several hours, we would go out for lunch. Mom always paid for the food, and I didn't object. She knew my situation, and the fact that we were cutting back on our spending. Mom wanted to help in whatever small way she could. I think it made her feel good to buy me lunch on those Saturdays and before I dropped her off, I always remembered to thank her.

****

One day in early February I spoke with some of my teacher friends at the middle school. They told me that the new associate principal at the middle school was extremely busy dealing with student discipline, teacher observations, and other day-to-day issues.

Although we had five associates at the high school, we were also kept very busy each day. We had over 2,200 students, many of whom needed our attention throughout the day. There were not only student discipline issues, but also student supervision duties before school, in the hallways between classes, during several lunch periods, and after school.

There was also a new teacher evaluation system being put into place that required numerous classroom visits from the administrators. With almost 100 teachers on staff, this took quite a bit of time out of our day to make these visits, and then document our observations. As I was pondering all this on my drive home a thought entered my mind. I decided to have a conversation with Debra the following day.

As planned, the next morning I walked to Debra's office and closed the door. "I have an idea," I told her. We discussed the new teacher evaluation system and how much time it was adding to the associate principals' day. I thought that a possible solution to this problem would be to have a 50/50 administrator. This person would spend half of their time at the middle school and half of their time at the high school. Their sole job could be doing teacher evaluations, or it could involve other responsibilities.

I told Debra that I would be perfect for that job! Having had experience at both levels, and also having done quite a bit of student discipline and teacher observations, it made total sense. I asked her if she would bring it up with Troy and/or Maude next time she saw them. She seemed to like the idea - or at least was pretending to - and promised to bring it up.

A couple of weeks later Debra told me that my idea had been shot down. I wasn't surprised, but I was disappointed.

* *

Although there had been rumblings about me leaving the high school, very few people had approached me with the topic – until now. February is the month in which educators begin talking about their contracts for the following year. Emails are sent from District Office to teachers and staff informing them of upcoming important dates - the deadline for submitting a retirement notification, the date in which contracts will be sent out, and the deadline for returning the signed contracts.

With all the chatter about next year, questions began to surface about my tenure. Teachers and staff approached me, wondering where I'd be the following year. I wasn't sure what I was supposed to tell people, so I checked with the Human Resources administrator. Remembering all too well my meeting with Maude, in which she chastised me for sharing information, I didn't want to get in trouble for saying the wrong thing. I was told that it was all right to acknowledge the fact that I wouldn't be at the high school next year due to administrative restructuring.

When people asked me if I would be working in the district, I honestly told them that I didn't know. Naively, I was still hoping for an administrative position within the district. I was so dumb but hope has a way of blinding us to reality.

I quickly realized how uncomfortable these conversations were becoming. I felt very sad about my situation, and having numerous people approach me each day with questions did not help my state of mind. I tried to keep the talk about my position to a minimum. When questioned, I'd change the subject or just reply, "I don't know." I don't blame these people for questioning me. They were not doing it to obtain gossip; they respected me and were concerned about my future.

* *

As Valentine's Day approached, announcements were made promoting the sale of "candy grams." This was an annual Student Council fundraising event – and a great excuse to sell candy at school. Over the past several years, the school district's Wellness Committee had made some significant changes in the food and drinks allowed at school. Despite the grumblings of faculty and students who wanted the freedom to choose either wisely or foolishly, all soda and candy vending machines had been removed from cafeterias and teacher's lounges. These unhealthy items were also taken out of school stores. This made the sale of candy grams even more special; it was the only time candy could be sold at school.

So for two weeks prior to Valentine's Day, Student Council members set up a table in the cafeteria and sold candy grams. Interested buyers could pick a flavored sucker, write a short note to the recipient, pay a dollar and have the candy gram delivered on Valentine's Day. Students bought them for their friends, for their teachers, and even for themselves.

February 14 arrived and with it came an air of excitement at school. Many staff and students wore pink or red in celebration of the holiday. Young men gave their girlfriends small stuffed animals, or flowers, which were proudly carried around all day for everyone to see.

The candy grams were delivered during third hour. And so began the sugar highs! The normally taboo candy was everywhere. Students debated about which flavor was the best. Besides the typical sucker flavors there was root beer, bubble gum, caramel apple, and cotton candy, to name a few. The smell of these sugary flavors filled the hallways and cafeteria. Everyone was in a good mood.

The flower shop van made several stops at the high school that day, delivering flowers for staff and students. Throughout our married life, Boyd would occasionally send me flowers. I might get them on Valentine's Day, our anniversary, or my birthday. When I completed my Master's Degree, he sent me flowers. And, once or twice I got an arrangement with an "I'm sorry" note attached.

But I knew there would be no flowers delivered for me on this day. Boyd and I had already begun talking about cutting back financially. We realized that we might be down to one income in the not-too-distant future, and buying flowers seemed like a waste of money. We had also decided not to exchange cards or gifts, and we ate dinner at home. What mattered was that we were together and happy in our marriage, even though we knew that a dark cloud was drifting closer to us.

13

MARCH 2012
NO WARMTH
ANYWHERE IN SIGHT

Federal Unemployment Rate: 8.2%
Total Number of Jobs Applied For: 10
Total Number of Interviews: 0

In the life of an educator, March is a great month. The reason for this is because with March comes spring break.

When staff and students return to school after the Christmas holiday, there are typically no days off until spring break. January and February seem to drag on forever. The only possibility of a day off is a snow day, and those don't occur very often. Having an entire week off in March is anticipated and appreciated by educators and students alike. Everyone is ready for a break before the end of school rush.

By March our skin is pale, and the cold winter weather seems as if it's never going to break. Many northerners travel south for spring break and, on occasion, our family is no exception.

For many years my parents wintered in Naples, renting a large two-bedroom condo for three to four months. Even after my dad died, mom continued to spend her winters in Florida until her health declined.

On several occasions, our family traveled to Naples to spend spring break with my parents. It was an affordable trip because our lodging was free. The Florida visit also allowed us to escape the cold temperatures and soak up the sun for a few days. We cherished these trips.

This spring break, however, we would not be going anywhere. We had money in our savings account but did not dare take any out for a vacation. We knew we might need that money once my paychecks stopped at the end of June.

With no vacation on our schedule, we spent the week cooped up in the house. It was too early, and too cold, to do yard work. We still had snow piled on the grass next to our driveway. I ended up sleeping in each morning, catching up on my rest. The majority of my days were spent worrying about the future.

I checked online, weekly, for administrative job openings in our area. Surprisingly, there were none listed yet. I prayed that something would open up soon because my time to find new employment was swiftly passing.

For the millionth time, I wondered whether I had made the correct choice a year ago, when Maude initially summoned me to her office. The stress of it all was eating away at me. Deep down, I knew that God had a plan for me; that he had directed me in my decision. It was just so difficult waiting to find out what His plan might entail.

My already high stress level during spring break would increase after a conversation that occurred with another employee of the school district.

14

APRIL 2012
I MAY NEVER KNOW

Federal Unemployment Rate: 8.1%
Total Number of Jobs Applied For: 10
Total Number of Interviews: 0

Once spring break is over, it seems as if the remainder of the school year flies by. Teachers are trying to get through the necessary curriculum and preparations are being made for graduation and summer school. There is an excitement in the air brought about by warmer weather and the knowledge that summer is just around the corner.

At the end of April our high school traditionally has a final pep rally. It's meant to be a celebration of a successful school year. The band plays several rousing tunes, spring sport athletes are recognized, and several student groups address the crowd, reminiscing about the highlights of the past school year. There are also several competitive games that take place pitting the different grade levels and faculty members against each other, including musical chairs, relay races, and a dance off.

As I stood off to the side, observing the festivities, and keeping an eye on the crowd, I felt a weight descend upon my chest. This would be my LAST pep rally. Once again I had to fight back tears. I struggled to hide my sadness. The end of my time at the high school was near and it seemed to be approaching at lightning speed.

Throughout these last months, I worked just as hard as I had before the bad news had been delivered to me. I was not going to let my horrible situation affect my job performance. I cared too much for the staff and students to give any less than 100% every day in which I had left.

* *

One day as I was walking down the hall at the high school, a custodian stopped me and said, "I think what the district is doing to you is so wrong." I didn't comment. He then told me his theory as to why I was being laid off. It was all political...

In early 2011, Wisconsin's governor, announced that in order to balance the state budget, public employees' collective bargaining rights needed to be taken away. The ensuing reaction by Wisconsin's teachers, firemen, policemen, and other public employees made national news for months. Numerous rallies took place at the capitol building in Madison.

Being lifelong educators, Boyd and I decided to attend one of these rallies. We wanted Kayla to share in the experience too – it was history in the making. So on a cold, snowy Saturday in March, we picked up Kayla in Milwaukee and then traveled to Madison for one of these rallies. There were tens of thousands of people present, inside and outside the capitol building. We walked through the crowds and listened to the speakers, taking it all in. We had never experienced anything like this before and, being a family who enjoyed "people-watching," found the whole thing very interesting.

On another occasion I rode on a bus down to Madison with Boyd and other educators for a smaller rally. I was an administrator, but didn't consider what I was doing as treasonous or a betrayal to the school district. The changes our governor was proposing affected all educators - teachers and administrators.

The custodian speculated that district personnel had gotten wind of the fact that I had attended rallies in Madison and were not happy about it. Upon hearing his theory I was filled with anxiety as questions filled my mind. Could that be it? Is that the real reason I'm being laid off? Who would have told Maude?

It wasn't as if I was going around school spouting off my political beliefs. I listened when others spoke about the situation, but never shared my views at school. I attended the rallies outside of my workday. According to the First Amendment, we all have the right to peaceably assemble. It's illegal to layoff an employee due to their political affiliation. If the district administrators were ticked off at me for attending the rallies, they weren't going to tell me.

I thought about the custodian's theory, off and on, for a few weeks. It seemed as good a reason as any as to how I ended up on Maude's bad side. At times I thought he might be right, but realized I would never know.

* *

Something that helped me keep my sanity during all this was yard work. I have always loved being outdoors, working in the yard. Throughout our marriage it had always been me who mowed the lawn. Our neighbors liked to give Boyd a hard time about that.

During the month of April, when temperatures in the 50s felt like a heat wave, I was able to get outside and start my spring yard work. I raked the grass in the front and backyard and prepared my garden for the following month's planting. For whatever reason, working in the yard has always calmed me. I put my iPod in my pocket, place the ear buds in my ears and escape with the work and my music.

If someone were to look at my playlist they would find music spanning many decades. Some of the artists from the past include The Cowsills, The Association, and Strawberry Alarm Clock, all popular in the 1960s. Fleetwood Mac, The Eagles, and Huey Lewis, as well as some "guilty pleasure" groups, also exist on my iPod. Some of those include The Bee Gees, Air Supply, Little River Band, Bread, and The Carpenters. I'm a sucker for a love song. Before I misrepresent myself, I must say that my iPod consists of several artists from the 21st century. Some of these include Green Day, Coldplay, The Click Five, and Chris Brown. I guess I can sum up my music choices as widely varied.

So between yard work and my beloved music, I was able to maintain at least a semblance of sanity – at least while at home. That mood would be challenged again very soon.

15

MAY 2012
ONE LAST KICK IN THE GUT

Federal Unemployment Rate: 8.2%
Total Number of Jobs Applied For: 12
Total Number of Interviews: 0

My job search picked up again in May. I had been checking the educational job posting websites throughout the spring months, however, there had been no openings in my area of the state until recently. In May I found two administrative openings relatively close to home. One of the openings was for a middle school principal; the other was for an elementary principal. Back in March I had requested updated letters of recommendation from several of my current and former supervisors. I also updated my resume and other application materials to reflect information from my second year at the high school. I applied for these two new positions, submitted my updated materials, and waited to hear from these school districts.

* *

By this time the entire staff knew that I would be leaving the district at the end of June. Daily, people stopped me in the halls or popped into my office to let me know their feelings. Some were mad, saying things like, "You're one of the best administrators I've worked with. What is the district thinking?" Others were sympathetic, telling me how sorry they were that I was leaving.

At one point my assistant came into my office and closed the door. Our eyes met, and without saying anything, we both burst into tears. We had worked together for two years and had developed a close relationship.

I received many thank you cards and some "best of luck" cards. All of these had touching, handwritten messages inside. It was all very overwhelming. I felt the caring support from staff, and that meant the world to me. I found myself on the verge of tears constantly. People were being so kind – it was a very emotional time.

* *

One morning toward the end of May I heard Troy's voice outside my office; he was talking to my assistant. I immediately got that, now familiar, heavy feeling of dread in my chest. My stress level went through the roof as I asked myself, "What now?" It couldn't be good – I had begun to expect bad news each time I saw him.

The week before, our district had announced that one of our elementary principals was retiring. Having been an elementary principal in the district, I had emailed our Human Resources department, letting them know I was interested in the position. I thought it would be a great opportunity to stay in the district (I was still holding out hope). They got back with me saying they were just beginning the search and more information would follow.

I greeted Troy and we entered my office. As he closed the door my throat closed along with it. Here it comes…more bad news.

"How is your job search going?" Troy asked, smiling at me as if nothing was wrong.

"I've applied for several positions in the area," I guardedly responded.

Troy then folded his hands in his lap, looked me in the eyes, and said, "I know that you are interested in the elementary principal position. There are also several available teaching positions at the elementary and middle school levels."

Then the bombshell was dropped.

"I want to let you know that you will not be considered for any of these positions in the district," is what I barely heard Troy say.

My ears were ringing and I felt as if I was going to faint. I was shocked and confused. Struggling to keep my composure, I asked, "Why will I not be considered for any jobs in the district?"

"It's because of the confidentiality issue," he responded.

I didn't know what to say. I couldn't think. Sitting in stunned silence, I tried to make sense of what I had just heard. I looked down at the papers on my desk, but the words swam in front of my eyes. I could feel Troy's eyes boring into me.

We sat in silence while I processed the information. Then it hit me and I said, "I will be unemployed in one month from now."

With that uncomfortable statement hanging in the air, Troy stood up to leave – but I didn't want him to go. I had something important to say but I couldn't put my thoughts together. He reached out to shake my hand and said, "Good luck to you in your job search."

Barely looking at Troy, I shook his hand but did not stand up or say anything. I couldn't think. Something wasn't right, but my mind was swimming and I couldn't focus on a single word.

Troy had delivered the news to me in a straightforward manner with seemingly little compassion or emotion. He had spent less than five minutes in my office. Although somewhere in the back of my mind I had known this scenario was a possibility, I couldn't believe what I had just heard. Something was wrong but I couldn't put my finger on it.

I sat at my desk feeling like I'd just been kicked to the curb – again. I consider myself a strong woman, however, at that moment I felt beaten down. Any self-confidence that I still possessed was shattered.

It wasn't until later, after I'd had time to totally process the conversation, that I figured out what hadn't made sense to me. Troy had told me that the reason I would not be considered for any job in the district was because of the confidentiality issue. But teachers aren't privy to any confidential information. And yet, I was not going to be given the opportunity to even teach in the district. The reason he gave me made no sense. That meant there was something else going on in which I was not aware.

Questions filled my mind. What could I have done that was so bad they did not want me working in the district? Was Maude the only one upset with me? Could it really be because I attended a couple of rallies in Madison? Looking at it from a different viewpoint I asked myself, Am I too strong of an administrator? Am I intimidating to Maude? I didn't know what to think. All I knew, for sure, was that in a few short weeks it would all be over. I would be moving out of my office and leaving the district for good. Once again the question I had asked months before entered my mind. Does 15 years of loyalty and dedication mean nothing to this school district? I had received the definitive answer that morning.

* *

The annual Scholarship Awards Program took place a few days after my meeting with Troy. This program is one of the highlights of the school year for senior students and their families. It is held in the spacious school auditorium and draws a crowd each year. Teachers, administrators, and community members present dozens of scholarships to the students. The presenters sit backstage, in order of appearance, until it's their turn to walk on stage to give their award.

As people were congregating backstage, I once again, put on a brave face and acted as if there was nothing wrong. A colleague and friend of mine approached me and asked how I was doing. In a hushed voice I informed her of my recent meeting with Troy. She couldn't believe the news and was puzzled as to why this was happening. Just then Maude walked in, and looked in our direction, so we went our separate ways. It was very sad, but I felt like I would get my friend in trouble if we continued a conversation.

Maude walked around backstage, greeting staff members and the public, with friendly handshakes and a big smile. I did my best to avoid her - not even making eye contact. It wasn't hard avoiding her; I felt as if she was doing the same with me. I was so hurt and confused, but I didn't want her to see it, so I put on a fake smile and made small talk with the people sitting close to me.

At one point in the evening, I looked across the room and noticed that Troy was looking at me. I was surprised by the look I saw in his eyes.

If I was reading him correctly, it almost seemed as if he felt sorry for me – quite a different feeling than I had gotten when he was breaking the news to me in my office. As soon as our eyes met, Troy quickly looked away.

As I sat backstage, waiting for my turn, I began to think that maybe Troy's role had been as the messenger. Maybe he had to act disconnected and uncaring in the meetings because he was just doing his job. Maybe he sympathized with my situation after all. It was just one more thing I might never know.

After the program was over and the backstage area was cleaned up, I left right away. Some of the other administrators were going out for a few drinks but I wasn't up for it at all. The closer it got to the end of the school year, the more of a recluse I became. It was difficult to keep my feelings hidden in front of these people. We were running out of things to talk about, since most conversations were work-related.

It was easier to just go home.

* *

With the reality of my situation crystal clear, I began to rely more and more on my faith. I had never been laid off of a job before, and thinking about what the coming months might bring scared me. Despite my fears, I felt strongly that God had a plan for me. There was a reason I had gotten laid off and I was confident that something better was just around the corner.

I found myself praying more than I had in quite some time. Often my prayers were just a sentence or two, asking God to help me get through the day. At night, as I lay in bed, inevitably thinking about my unknown future, I let God know that I trusted Him with whatever path He planned for me to take. My faith truly helped me get through some of the toughest days I had ever faced.

16

JUNE 2012
FINAL FEW DAYS

Federal Unemployment Rate: 8.2%
Total Number of Jobs Applied For: 17
Total Number of Interviews: 0

The first week of June was the last week of school for Boyd and me. The last week of school consists of final exams, entering final grades, and the high school graduation ceremony.

This year's graduation – my first, and my last - was on a Thursday evening. Having finished their exams the day before, seniors had the morning off. They were required, however, to attend graduation practice during the afternoon. Throughout the rehearsal there was excitement in the air. Graduation was an end for the seniors, but it was also a beginning. For some of them, this realization was starting to take hold.

That evening, during the ceremony, James and I supervised the students as they entered the field house and walked to their seats. That placed us toward the back of the room. I ended up sitting alone in the last row, behind a row of teachers. I felt inconspicuous, which was exactly what I wanted. None of the seniors sitting in front of me knew that, like them, I would also be leaving the high school very soon.

As I watched the ceremony, I asked God to guide the graduates in their future endeavors, whether it be more schooling or in the workforce. I also asked Him to guide me in the upcoming months. Whichever path He wanted me to travel, I would go willingly.

After the ceremony, all the high school administrators posed for a picture on stage. As I stood there with my fake smile, I wondered, "Why am I even in this picture?" Deep down I knew I had been a positive influence on many students over the past two years, and I was respected by the high school staff. I just felt so beaten down by the district administrators. My self-confidence was at an all-time low.

Many staff members, as well as the high school administrators, went out for a post-graduation celebration at a local bar. I went home.

* *

The following morning was the Retirees' Breakfast. It was also the last day I would see teachers and other staff members. The significance of the situation did not escape me. I felt close to tears from the moment I arrived at school that day.

As I entered the cafeteria I noticed that Maude was not there, however, Troy was in attendance, representing the district administration. I was flooded with relief. With my emotions so raw I did not want to see Maude.

I got a cup of coffee and some fruit and sat down with the other associate principals. They could tell I wasn't doing well and knew not to bring up any touchy subjects.

Max said, "Hey Nancy, we missed you last night."

I just nodded, giving no excuse. They knew why I hadn't attended.

After the welcome speech, given by Troy, the retirees gave their speeches. That was followed by the annual presentation of the "Friends of the Police Department" award. Our Police School Liaison Officer, Peter, presents this award to a staff member or an administrator who has gone over and above to help him out during the school year. I had won this award while I was an assistant principal at the middle school and was anxious to hear who the recipient would be this year.

Peter started his presentation describing what the award meant. Then I heard him say, "I'm happy to announce that this year's recipient is Nancy Chessman!" What? I had won the award? I looked at the other associate principals in shock. They were nodding their heads, affirming that I had heard correctly. I stood and walked up to the podium in a daze.

I had only known Peter for two years but we had developed a friendship very quickly. He had an amazing sense of humor and, along with the associate principals, had welcomed me to the high school with open arms. Peter and I had not only a great working relationship, but also a great respect for one another.

As I approached the podium, Peter gave me a big hug. I felt tears well up in my eyes. Peter then began to say many nice things about me; how well I worked with students in trouble, how I'd assisted him on many occasions. It was a struggle to hold my emotions inside. I was so grateful that Peter had wanted me to receive this honor. I knew that part of the reason was because it was my last year in the school district but that didn't matter. It was his way of saying I was appreciated and would be missed.

When Peter finished there was a roar of applause from the high school staff members. Holding back my tears was no longer an option. I felt the gratitude and the compassion from everyone in the room. For a moment I actually wished Maude had been there to see all the support I was given. As I walked back to my seat, plaque in hand, I passed Troy. He was smiling at me and nodding as if to convey, "You deserve the award and the appreciation."

Throughout the remainder of the breakfast I was a mess. After the speeches had concluded people mingled, wishing each other a long, restful summer. Many people approached me to say good-bye. It felt as if I was at my own funeral. Every time someone hugged me the tears started up again. Finally, I had to go back to my office so I could calm down. My eyes were red and puffy and I needed to stop crying.

* *

Knowing my last paycheck would be at the end of June, Boyd and I, once again, had a discussion about our finances. As an administrator, I was making more than Boyd. That meant our income would be cut by over one half. With Kayla in college, that was a scary thought. We had one asset that we were willing to sell to help make ends meet – our travel trailer.

We had owned the travel trailer for ten years. In that time we had traveled north to Canada, south to Florida, east to the Carolinas, and west to South Dakota and Wyoming, pulling our mobile home behind us. Boyd, Kayla, and I had created so many great family memories in that travel trailer. The thought of selling it was sad, but with Kayla gone we weren't using it as much as we had in the past.

In April I had put an ad on Craigslist. We had kept the travel trailer in great condition and were asking a fair price. At first we had many inquiries; two couples even came to look at it, but no one was interested in buying. After a month had passed we received an email from a newlywed couple from Canada. Numerous emails were exchanged, questions were asked and answered, more pictures were sent, and the price was negotiated. They decided to buy our travel trailer and were going to drive down, arriving on Friday, June 15, to pick it up. Coincidentally, June 15 also happened to be my last day of work.

****

After 15 years of service, there was only one week left before I would leave the school district for good. I had gotten permission from Debra to take vacation days during the last two weeks of June. The Human Resources department had let me know that I could only get paid for five unused vacation days. Therefore, I wanted to use all but those five days – I was not about to leave anything on the table.

The beginning of that last week brought summer school, which kept me busy for a few days. I took time to go through files, bookshelves, and my desk. My diplomas and pictures came down off the walls and boxes were filled with my personal things. By Friday, my office was bare and I had little to do.

The other high school administrators were going to take me out to lunch on my last day as a final farewell. At about 11:30 a.m. Boyd called me saying the couple from Canada was almost to our house. We hadn't expected them to pick up the travel trailer until late afternoon, but they were making good time. I needed to get home right away.

With much haste I sent a text to the other administrators, letting them know I would not be able to make lunch. I received a text from

Debra saying we would reschedule for the following week. I then gave my assistant a final hug, grabbed the last box, and walked out of the high school for the last time.

There were no tears as I drove away from the school toward home. I did not feel guilty leaving a few hours early. I had given so many extra hours to that school district over the years; one afternoon off didn't come close to making up that time.

It was almost a relief that it was finally over. I had known for 14 months that this day would come. I didn't feel anger. I didn't feel sadness. If anything, I felt empty. For the first time in 15 years I had no idea what my future held.

* *

Once school was over, I applied for five administrative positions, all within about 30 miles of our home. One of the openings was at a middle school in which I knew the principal. I called her to let her know I was interested in the associate principal position at her school. I had to leave a message because she had not answered her phone. A few days later I tried calling her again, this time speaking with her assistant. The assistant told me she was out of town for a few days so I left another message. She never called me back and I did not get an interview. For that matter, I didn't have any interviews in June. I was beginning to wonder if my name was being blackballed by the administration in my school district. I hoped that was not the case.

* *

By mid-June Boyd was already a week into his summer break. At the end of the school year, teachers as well as students, are ready to relax and enjoy some much-needed time off. He couldn't wait to get out on his boat and do some fishing. During the summers Boyd went fishing three to four times a week. When he wasn't out on the lake he was either on a tennis court or a golf course.

As a school administrator, I hadn't had a summer off in five years. With everything I had gone through over the past year, I was looking forward to some free time. Sleeping past 5:00 a.m. in the morning, soaking up some sun on the boat, and working on projects around the house sounded like heaven. In June of 2012, I was confident that by autumn I would have a job. I couldn't have been more wrong.

17

JULY 2012
THE EMBARRASSMENT
OF UNEMPLOYMENT

Federal Unemployment Rate: 8.3%
Total Number of Jobs Applied For: 23
Total Number of Interviews: 2

July 1, 2012 was my first official day of unemployment. Boyd and I had discussed whether or not I should file for unemployment benefits. Several of my colleagues told me that I had every right to collect unemployment. I had been laid off by the school district and since my last paycheck was in June, we needed some kind of income to help pay our bills. The decision was made – I would apply. Neither Boyd nor I had ever needed to collect unemployment, so the whole process was new to me.

During the last week in June I called the Wisconsin Department of Workforce Development (DWD) to inquire about applying for unemployment. I was so embarrassed making that phone call. I had three degrees and, until now, had earned a decent wage. Regretfully, this was something I had to do, no matter how humiliating it might be.

I not only felt embarrassment – I also felt guilt. There were so many people in more dire circumstances than me who needed unemployment benefits. We still had our home, three vehicles, a small boat, and food on the table. I told myself it would only be for a couple of months and we could use the help in paying our bills.

The DWD woman answered my questions and told me I could apply online. Since I was on vacation until the end of June, my unemployment benefits would not start until July. I found out there is a "waiting week" in which I would not collect payment. That meant I would not be receiving an unemployment check until the second week of July. That was all right – it wasn't as if we had no income. Even though he didn't work during the summer, Boyd's salary was paid evenly throughout the entire year.

I received an envelope full of information from the DWD a few days later. In order to receive weekly benefits, I would have to go online and fill out a "Weekly Claim Certification" each week. This claim certification involved answering eleven yes/no questions about availability to work, whether any income was earned that week, and whether I had applied for two jobs. That was one stipulation of receiving unemployment – applying for two jobs each week was required. I wondered how many people were cheating the system with this requirement. It would be very easy to lie about applying for jobs, especially since it was online.

The informational packet I received explained that, at any time, I might be required to show proof of the jobs for which I had applied. They even supplied a form I was to use to record this information. Being a good citizen, I made copies of the necessary form and read through the rest of the information they had sent to me.

Another interesting fact about unemployment benefits is that there is a maximum dollar amount a person can collect each week. My salary as an Associate Principal had been high enough to put me at the maximum amount. I would receive a check for $363 each week. I did some figuring and realized that was approximately one-fourth of what I used to make. That was a very depressing piece of information. Our discussions on cutting back our expenditures began again in earnest.

* *

For many years we had the luxury of a cleaning lady. Most people with a house cleaner have them come every week or every other week. We justified the expense by only having her come to clean once a month. In our 25 years of marriage, I had done the majority of the cleaning. When Boyd and I got married I told him that I would do all the cleaning and the laundry if he would agree to do the one chore I hated – cleaning the bathrooms. What was I thinking? I was young and in love and stupid. I've already told Kayla not to make the same mistake I did. Always share the chores evenly!

Boyd actually began helping more with household tasks when I went back to school for my Educational Leadership degree. He would vacuum or empty the dishwasher; he even made a few meals. Kayla also had some assigned chores while she was growing up, so I did have a certain amount of help around the house.

When our cleaning lady came at the end of June I let her know that I had been laid off and that we would need to put her services on hold until I found another job. I told her I'd probably be calling her in a couple of months to resume her monthly duties. That was the first of many changes in our spending habits.

We decided to cut way back on dining out. It didn't seem like we went out that much, however, with my working hours as an administrator longer than they were as a teacher, there were times when I'd pick something up on the way home, or we'd go out. Now, it was relatively easy to prepare meals at home because I was no longer working. I had more time to think about what to make - which is half the battle – and then prepare it. One day Boyd commented that we were running our dishwasher much more often than in the past. I told him it was because we were eating three meals a day at home. Since one of his jobs was emptying the dishwasher, this chore was keeping him busy.

Besides the spending cuts we had already made, we knew we needed to do more. After pondering on this for a few days, Boyd came up with some good ideas. He called our auto insurance company and spoke with our agent about raising our deductibles and lowering our cost. They were able to decrease our monthly car insurance expense by about $40 a month. Boyd also called the cable company and reduced our services, which reduced that bill.

I was doing my part too. I began clipping coupons from our grocery store's advertisements. While grocery shopping, I actually looked at the cost of the items I was putting in my basket. I hate to admit it, but it had been many years since I had done that.

Being an avid Kohls department store shopper – and credit card holder - I received monthly coupons for 15%, 20%, or 30% off. In the past, whenever I received a 30% off coupon, I felt obligated to use it. Even if there was nothing that I needed at the time, I couldn't resist taking advantage of the discount. Now, if a 30% off coupon came in the mail, I took a deep breath and... threw it away. I felt very proud of my newfound willpower.

One day, after walking the dog, I was taking off my sneakers and noticed how worn down they had become. I really needed new walking shoes but didn't want to spend the money. Then I remembered that mom had given me $100 last month for my birthday. I had tucked the money away, in the bottom of a drawer, and had totally forgotten about it.

So with cash in my pocket, I headed out buy myself some new shoes. I went to several stores, comparing prices. With the exception of large purchases - furniture, appliances, television sets - I had not comparison shopped for years. However, with our current situation, I wanted to find a sturdy pair of shoes for the least possible amount of money.

I ended up finding a pair of walking shoes in my size on the clearance rack. I liked the way they looked and they were comfortable. The best part was that they were only $50. I couldn't wait to share my thriftiness with Boyd!

* *

Every Sunday or Monday I would open up our aging laptop computer and go online to the DWD web site. Once there I would answer the required eleven questions in order to receive unemployment benefits for the week. I thought it would become easier to apply for this financial help after a few weeks - it didn't. Following that task I would go to the websites for job opportunities in education. By this time I had bookmarked all the aforementioned sites.

I applied for at least two jobs each week. The majority of the openings were for building administrators, however, I didn't limit myself to applying for only Principal or Associate Principal positions. I did not have the luxury of being picky at this point. I began to apply for Dean of Students openings. A Dean is not quite an administrator but is a step up from a teacher. Deans spend most of their day handling student discipline and supervising students, during lunch hours and before and after school. I also applied for jobs with other educational agencies in Wisconsin that support school districts.

As luck would have it, I received a phone call requesting a prescreening telephone interview from the Wisconsin RtI Center. RtI stands for Response to Intervention. It is a process used in schools to help students achieve higher levels of academic and behavioral success. They were looking for someone with a strong math background to assist area school districts in implementing RtI within each of their schools.

I immediately began to prepare for the interview, doing research online and speaking with former colleagues who were well versed in RtI. A few days later, after kicking Boyd out of the house, I had my phone interview. It only lasted about 20 minutes but I felt it had gone well. The woman I had spoken with let me know that second round, in-person interviews, would be held soon and I would be hearing from them, either way, within a few days.

Needless to say, the next few days were torture. Every time the phone rang I wondered if it was the Wisconsin RtI Center calling. Much to my delight, four days after my telephone interview, I received a phone call from the RtI Center to schedule a second round interview. After the call was over I was ecstatic. The next few days were spent preparing and praying.

Although this was not a traditional job in education, I wondered if this was God's plan for me. Was I supposed to get this job so I could help dozens of school districts and thousands of students? I let God know that if this were the road He wanted me to travel, I would go willingly.

During the same week I received a call for another interview. I had applied for a High School Principal position in a small school district about 30 miles from home. The Superintendent of this district knew me and knew my current situation. She had worked in my former school district several years ago. I was sure the only reason I was getting an interview was because of my acquaintance with this woman. I was ok with that – at the very least I would get some interview practice. If I were lucky enough to get the job, that would be even better.

Now I was preparing for two interviews that would take place during the same week. My interview for the High School Principal position was on Monday and my second round interview with the RtI Center was on Thursday. With an optimism I hadn't felt in months, I got to work.

In preparation for the first interview, I researched the school district and the high school and practiced dozens of possible interview questions. As I drove to the high school I reviewed these questions and practiced my answers out loud. Anyone looking at me while I was driving probably wondered whom I was talking to since I was alone! My nerves were working overtime; this would be my first in-person interview outside of my previous school district in 15 years.

When I arrived for the interview I was placed in a room and was given about 30 minutes to handwrite an answer to one of three questions. Districts like to do this to make sure the candidate has appropriate writing and grammatical skills, as well as an ability to put their thoughts into words. By the time I was finished writing my answer, my right hand was throbbing.

Next, I was taken to a classroom for the actual interview. As I walked into the room I saw a panel of about a dozen people sitting behind a row of tables. They were all facing a table with a single chair in which I was invited to sit. My stomach felt like it was in my throat. I was offered a bottle of water and gratefully accepted. The panel members introduced themselves to me; there were administrators, teachers, parents, and even a student. The Superintendent sat at the end of the group. Her familiar face gave me a modicum of comfort.

Over the next 90 minutes I answered their questions. There weren't any surprise questions and when it was all over I felt confident in my performance. I was told that there would be second round interviews granted to two people the following week. I would hear back from them either way.

Three days after my interview for the High School Principal job, I was headed for my second in-person interview. I had been told that there would be two women conducting this interview. After answering questions from a dozen people this would be a piece of cake. Once again, throughout the interview I felt confident in my answers and pictured myself doing the job. There would be quite a bit of travel, however, much of the time I would be working at home. That thought appealed to me.

On my drive home I was on Cloud Nine. They had told me that they would be interviewing one other person. That meant I was a finalist. I was sure I would get the job. It was perfect timing. I would be starting in mid-August. That meant I could stop filing for unemployment benefits after only six weeks. I formulated in my mind the email I would send to my former colleagues, letting them know of my new position.

My confidence was so high that I spent the next few days reorganizing our in-home office. After all, I would be spending more time in this room when I started working for the RtI Center. Having only one child, we had converted one of the extra bedrooms in our home into an office. I used it when paying bills, doing our income taxes, and when working on the laptop. While I organized and thoroughly cleaned the office I said numerous prayers, asking God to grant me this job.

Eight days after my interview for the High School Principal position, the Superintendent called me to let me know they had conducted second round interviews and had selected another candidate. She told me that several members of the panel had ranked me as their number one choice. In spite of this, other candidates had been chosen because the majority of the panel had picked them. I thanked her for the opportunity and disconnected. I didn't feel all that bad because I knew I was going to get the RtI position.

Days went by without any word from the Wisconsin RtI Center. With each passing day my confidence dwindled. Why had they not called me? Were they having difficulties contacting my references? I was so sure I was going to get the job. What was taking so long?

Finally, I decided to take the bull by the horns. I called one of the women with whom I had interviewed. She wasn't in but I left a message inquiring on the status of the job. It took her four more days to call me back. By this time my confidence was all but gone. When I finally heard from the woman, she let me know they had offered the position to the other finalist.

Two interviews. Two failures. At least that's how I interpreted it. I couldn't believe this was happening. My first reaction was shock, and then I was plunged into depression. I had convinced myself that I would get the job. I vowed to never make that mistake again. It took me days to drag myself out of the depression. I found myself praying many times each day. I needed God to help me get my head straight again.

* *

Boyd and I were invited to several parties during the summer of 2012. There were graduation parties of former students, a farewell party for a colleague who was moving away, and several happy hours. Although Boyd attended a few of the parties, I stayed at home. I was embarrassed and depressed about my situation and I did not feel like answering the same questions over and over. Seeing the looks of pity on all those faces was also a reason to stay home. Maybe it was cowardice on my part but I could not face my former colleagues. It was easier to hide out at home.

As July came to an end, Boyd began thinking about school starting up in another month. My thoughts revolved around the fact that I had less than a month to find a job. Boyd was getting up very early most mornings to go out on the lake while the fishing was the best. I would sleep in a bit, eat breakfast, take the dog for a walk, and then usually plop myself down in front of the television. I had completed the majority of the planned household projects and I wasn't very motivated to do much of anything.

Prior to July, I would equate the emotional rollercoaster ride I was on to a kiddie coaster, with gentle ups and downs and only a few curves. This month, I boarded a much larger rollercoaster. I had lived through a major rise, then an abrupt fall; the kind of fall in which you feel as if you are going to fly out of your seat, totally out of control. Unknown to me, my uncontrollable ride had just begun.

18

AUGUST 2012
CRUNCH TIME

Federal Unemployment Rate: 8.1%
Total Number of Jobs Applied For: 38
Total Number of Interviews: 2

It was crunch time. The pressure to find a job increased tenfold and my stress level was through the roof. They say that stress can be detrimental to your health. I was living proof of that – my stomach hurt all the time and I had difficulty sleeping.

Since I had no reason to get up in the morning I got into the bad habit of staying up way past midnight. I began to watch *Friends* reruns; Nick at Nite ran four episodes in a row starting at 10:00 p.m. Unlike most people, I hadn't watched *Friends* when it originally aired in the 1990s and early 2000s, so the series was new to me. I quickly became addicted but had a difficult time following the story lines. The episodes were run in random order, so at 10:00 Rachel was dating her personal shopping client Joshua, at 10:30 she was marrying Ross in Vegas, at 11:00 they weren't on speaking terms, and at 11:30 she was dating Tag. Despite the lack of chronology, I couldn't stop watching the show. The humor let me escape from my state of joblessness for two hours each night. It didn't take long before I had seen every episode. The reruns were now reruns for me too. That didn't matter – I still watched.

The reason I intentionally stayed up late was because I was trying to make myself as tired as possible so I could fall asleep when I finally went to bed. Unfortunately, that usually didn't work. When I went to bed my situation immediately came to mind, preventing any hope of sleep. I would lie there thinking: Why am I not getting called for interviews? Should I start looking for more jobs outside the realm of education?

Could I start my own business? What could I do? Become a personal shopper/errand runner? Cook and deliver dinners to busy households? Write a book? Write a children's book? Tutor struggling students in math? Do something online like blogging or writing?

Many of my ideas were ridiculous and would not allow me to earn the kind of money I was making as a school administrator. Despite that, I was desperate to get back to work and earn some money. That thought consumed me day and night.

I also used my sleeplessness as a time to pray. I was way past the, "God, I will travel whatever path you choose for me" prayers. I was now begging God for a job by the time school started. I questioned Him as to why He was having me go through this depressing, stressful situation. Deep down I knew He had something better planned for me and I implored Him to reveal that "something better" sooner rather than later.

I hadn't been a late sleeper since my college days. So whether I went to bed at 10:00 p.m. or 1:30 a.m., I still woke up before 8:00 a.m. the following morning. I'm also not a nap-taker so I was becoming sleep deprived. If I went to bed early I couldn't sleep. If I went to bed late I couldn't sleep. It was a vicious cycle.

* *

With a continued feeling of guilt, I applied for an unemployment check each week during the month of August. I kept telling myself that very soon I would be able to stop receiving the government's help. Every time I pressed the submit button I would think about other people needing unemployment benefits more than me; those living in tiny, run-down apartments, or the single moms with children to feed, or the people who had been looking for work for years without success.

Although we had eliminated almost all of our extra expenses, Boyd and I still needed the unemployment check to help us pay our bills. We had lived within our means throughout our married life, but we had always planned our expenses around our income. The situation we were currently experiencing was brand new to us. Neither one of us had ever been laid off or fired from a job before. We still had to make the house payment, a car payment, and pay our other monthly bills. The unemployment checks helped us make ends meet and kept us from using all our savings just to get by.

One day in early August I received a letter from the DWD telling me that, on August 16, I was required to attend a meeting at the local unemployment office. The meeting would cover topics including, how to find a job, how to network to find a job, and how to correctly fill out the Weekly Certification Form. The letter stated that I should bring proof of the jobs I'd applied for over the past two weeks. If I did not attend, my benefits would end.

I was immediately filled with dread. I did not want to go to this meeting. I already knew how to apply for jobs, I was networking to find a job, and I knew how to fill out the weekly form. The worst part about having to go to the meeting was the possibility of seeing someone who knew me. If that happened I would die of embarrassment.

That feeling of hatred toward Maude welled up in me again. For a reason I could not fathom, she is the one who put me in this dreadful situation.

As the 16th drew near, my anxiety increased. I had no choice. As much as I was dreading it, I had to go to the meeting. When I woke up that morning, it was raining. The weather mirrored my mood – dark and dismal. Since I had never been there, I had used MapQuest to get directions to the unemployment office, which was in a neighboring city. On my drive to the meeting I felt like throwing up. I looked over at the passenger seat to make sure I had grabbed the folder that contained the job application forms. The letter had said to bring forms for the last two weeks but since I'd only been on unemployment for six weeks, I choose to bring all the forms. I wanted them to know that I was seriously pursuing a job. I had also put my resume in the folder, just in case they wanted to look it over.

The office was tucked away behind a Goodwill store. Even with the MapQuest directions, the place was impossible to find. It was pouring rain and it was getting late. I finally found the office, parked the car in a spot that was not at all close to the building, grabbed the paperwork I was required to bring, and quickly ran through the rain. I tried to avoid the growing puddles however, in my rush, I stepped right into the middle of a pool of water, soaking my foot. Could this day get any worse?

I knew I was a couple of minutes late but there was nothing I could do about it now. When I entered the building, I stood there looking around. A horrible thought crossed my mind. Was I in the wrong place? With growing embarrassment, I approached a woman sitting at the reception desk.

"Where is the unemployment office?" I asked, praying I was in the correct place.

"It's at the other end of the building," she replied.

Oh no. I was already late; this would only make me later.

I then asked, "Do I have to go back outside and drive around the building or can I get to the office through the building?"

The woman pointed down a long hallway, "Go down this hallway, then turn left. The office will be on your right."

With that, I walked quickly down the hall, rain dripping off of my umbrella, and finally located the reception area for the unemployment office.

I approached the woman sitting behind the counter and, in a hushed voice I said, "My name is Nancy Chessman. I'm here for the unemployment meeting."

She immediately looked at the clock. My eyes followed hers. It was 9:04. I was four minutes late. She told me, "I'm not sure if they will let you in the meeting because you are late."

As she turned to her colleague to ask if it was too late for me to attend the meeting, my mind raced. This could not be happening. I said a quick prayer, asking God to let these women show me some mercy and let me attend. It was only four minutes; the presenters were probably still introducing themselves. I couldn't have missed much.

The second woman - who must have been some kind of supervisor - looked at me, and in a voice that scolded me for being late, said, "Go ahead and go in."

I sent God a quick thank you and headed toward the meeting room. The door was open and I saw about 30 people sitting at tables arranged in a horseshoe. Three presenters stood at the front of the room addressing the participants.

Wishing for invisibility, I walked into the room. I kept my head down so no one would recognize me. Being late, I had to visually search for a place to sit, and of course, everyone in the room looked up at the late arrival – me. Someone pointed out an empty chair and I quickly walked toward it, my head still down. I cannot express in words how embarrassed I was at that moment. Even after I took my seat, I dared not look up.

It took me a good five minutes before I looked around the room. There were men and women of all ages sitting around the table. Thankfully I didn't recognize anyone and no one was staring at me. Once again I asked God to give me the strength and the courage to get through the next two and a half hours.

As the presentation progressed, I was able to relax a bit. If I was going to be here for the rest of the morning, I might as well make the best of it. The information being shared was helpful and it reassured me that I was doing the right things to find a job. With about an hour left, we were informed that we would be taken out individually to speak with an employment counselor about our paperwork. Then came some news that made my stress level increase significantly.

We were going to go around the circle, and each of us was to share our unemployment situation. No! I just wanted to sit quietly and unnoticed, listen to the presentation, and go home. Thankfully they started on the opposite side of the table from where I was sitting. One by one, people explained what job they had had, why they had lost the job, and what they were doing to find a new position.

As each person spoke, others in the group would offer suggestions or give names of possible contact people. I saw the benefit of this activity – we were networking. Still, I prayed that when it was close to being my turn I'd be called out to do my individual meeting. I really did not want to share my story. Every time the counselor came in to call another person I prayed I would hear my name. Each time it was someone else. When there were only about five or six of us who hadn't had our individual meeting, I figured my name hadn't been called because I had arrived late. Whatever the reason, I was not going to get out of presenting my story.

Many of the people at this meeting had been laid off because of cutbacks at their former place of employment. There were factory and office workers, a photographer, a couple of people who worked in the hotel business, and several in food service. When it finally was my turn to speak, I kept it as short as possible.

I began by saying that my last job was as a High School Associate Principal. As soon as I said that, there were gasps throughout the room. I guess they were shocked that an unemployed educator was receiving unemployment benefits. Their reaction only intensified my embarrassment. I went on to say that I had been laid off due to budget cuts and that I was applying for other administrative positions. The presenter asked me a couple of questions that I answered. Then, thankfully, my turn was over.

We were supposed to be done by 11:30, but the individual meetings were taking longer than expected. I had to sit around and wait for my name to be called. Finally, I met with the counselor. She didn't have much to say because I was doing everything possible to find a job. It was noon before I was able to leave. I used my drive home to decompress and thank God for helping me through the morning.

* *

A few days after my unemployment meeting I was over at mom's apartment helping her go through some boxes that were stacked in her office. In order to expedite the process of emptying her house, we had brought several boxes to her apartment to go through at our leisure. Before we started our task I told her about the meeting I'd been required to attend earlier in the week. As I was explaining it to her I started crying. The weight of my situation, combined with telling my mom, was just too much. I hadn't cried in weeks, but the meeting had taken a toll on me and I guess I needed to let it out.

Mom said she was praying for me and that she felt confident that something would happen for me. Having a daughter myself, and knowing how much I hurt when she was hurting, I'm sure my mom was feeling my pain as well.

****

Each August, teachers across the nation begin preparing their classrooms for the upcoming school year. While I was still teaching, I would not only prepare my classroom but also help Boyd with his. He would say, "You do a much better job than me when it comes to putting up bulletin boards. You're so creative." We both knew that he was complimenting me so I would help him!

When Kayla got old enough, she loved to come with us to assist with arranging desks, putting up bulletin boards, and taping posters to the walls. Since I had become an administrator and worked for much of the summer, Kayla and Boyd had worked in his room. It was great father/daughter time. But, now that Kayla was living in Milwaukee and I was not working, Boyd asked if I would help him prepare his room again.

I hesitated in agreeing because I didn't want to run into anyone at the school. I had been the Assistant Principal there for two years and had taught with many of the teachers for 10 years before that. I also didn't want to run into the new Principal or Associate Principal. They would ask me if I had found a job yet, which I hadn't, and I would have to go through a long explanation.

In order to get me to come with him, Boyd agreed to my terms. We went to the school in the late afternoon – the hottest part of the day - when less people would be present. We parked inconspicuously and entered through a side door. Once we got to Boyd's classroom, we closed the door and turned on several fans. As most schools in Wisconsin, this one had no air conditioning. There were only a few weeks in the fall and, maybe a couple of weeks in the spring, when it was uncomfortably hot.

We worked in Boyd's room for about two hours. I put up a couple of bulletin boards and Boyd arranged his desk and his lab supplies. Together we rearranged the tables in the room until Boyd was satisfied with the setup. We only encountered one person that day - the custodian. Thankfully the conversation was short and the topic of my situation never came up.

As we drove away I reflected on how uncomfortable I had been at Boyd's school. How different the feelings were now, just two years after I had worked there. I used to feel happiness as I entered the building, looking forward to interacting with staff and students each day. Now, I feared walking through the door, dreading the possibility of running into someone. Sad as it was, if I had to be there, I just wanted to hide.

* *

Although I was only "required" to apply for two jobs a week, during the month of August I applied for 15 more jobs. I was very motivated to get a position for the quickly approaching school year. There were numerous administrative positions for which I applied, however, I also began to apply for middle school math teaching positions, math coaching positions, Dean of Students positions, and district-wide Math Coordinator positions. There was no room to be picky at this point.

There were many openings in the Milwaukee area for which I applied. Although it would mean living there during the week, apart from Boyd, at least Kayla would be close. She and I would be able to hang out on occasion – something she told me she'd love to do.

I was so desperate by August that I even applied for a Co-Directorship at a local preschool. When Kayla found out she said, "Mom, you can't stand little kids." OK, it's not that I can't stand preschoolers; I just don't like spending a lot of time with them. I would have a difficult time interacting with them all day, every day. Also, the pay for this job was just above minimum wage.

I was desperate.

Toward the end of the month I found an opening at a private college that had centers located throughout the state. One of the centers, located close to home, was looking for an Advisor/Center Coordinator. As I read the job description it sounded perfect for me. I had had some experience advising high school students and I had the leadership skills to successfully run the center.

A former teaching colleague of mine worked for the college as an instructor and department head. I searched for his phone number in my old school directories and gave him a call. We had been close friends about 10 years prior and I knew he would be willing to do whatever he could to help me get an interview. He gave me some more information about the job and told me he would speak with the human resources person. He let me know that the job only paid about $45,000 – quite a bit less than what I was making as an associate principal. It didn't matter. I needed a job, and $45,000 was better than $0.

I was confident that I would get an interview, but I never heard from the college.

One day, as I was searching the Internet for jobs, I noticed a posting for a Middle School Associate Principal position. It was at the school that Lexie's daughter (my former student) worked at – the school that had hired the PhD for the position the previous year. Wow! I knew that man wouldn't last in an AP position. After informing Lexie, I applied for the job for a second time. Lexie assured me that her daughter would put a good word in for me again. Once again, I did not hear a word.

* *

The beginning of the school year for teachers was only a week away and I didn't have a job. I was sick with worry. I had applied for so many jobs and had had only two interviews. I didn't know what I would do if I didn't find a position.

In late August, Kayla sent me a text saying her fall tuition was due. She let me know the amount, and the due date, which was quickly approaching. Even with financial aid, her tuition was substantial. Now that we had only one source of income, the amount was overwhelming.

Boyd and I had been putting money away for Kayla's college for many years. The designated amount was automatically withdrawn from our checking account each month and deposited into an Education Savings Account. We had stopped this automatic withdrawal during my last year of employment, just in case.

I transferred money out of the Education Savings Account and mailed the fall tuition check, noting the dwindling amount remaining in the account. Now that Kayla was out of the dorms, we did not have to pay the college for her room and board. Instead, we sent Kayla a check each month to cover her rent and other expenses. Fortunately, that amount was less than what we had paid when she lived in the dorms.

* *

As the school year drew closer, Boyd and I discussed the possibility of me getting a job as a substitute teacher. I had subbed when I first graduated from college 30 years ago. I hated it then, and knew I would hate it now. Nevertheless, I had to do something.

Being a substitute in my former school district was not an option. I had been an administrator at several schools in the district; returning as a substitute teacher would be humiliating. Additionally, I wasn't even sure they would allow me to sub in the district (Maude might be afraid of me leaking all of that confidential information that substitute teachers receive.). Since I had left with no clear idea of why I had been laid off, I was not going to permit them to deny me again. They had hurt me enough.

Reluctantly, I powered up the laptop and went to the website of a school district just to the north of our town. I found the information about how to apply to be a substitute teacher. There was a mountain of paperwork involved in the application process. I was overwhelmed. I didn't want to sub and it was going to be a gigantic hassle to apply. Exasperated, I shutdown the computer and walked away. I couldn't do this.

* *

On Tuesday, August 28, Boyd, and the hundreds of other staff members in my former school district, began their first day of fall in-service. Each year began with all district employees reporting to the high school auditorium for convocation. High school students would stand just outside the auditorium, forming a tunnel for staff members to walk through. The students cheered and applauded while everyone made their way into the auditorium.

Maude would start the morning with a 20 to 30 minute speech, followed by other district administrators and the board president giving short spiels. The human resources administrator then introduced new staff. After a short break, staff members would attend meetings by department or grade level.

When Boyd and I woke up this particular Tuesday morning, we were both on the verge of tears. For over a dozen years, we had both attended the first day convocation at the high school. Today, only Boyd would be there. I couldn't believe this was happening. Not only was I not attending my former school district's first day activities, I wasn't attending any school district's first day activities. For the first time in 30 years, I was not going to walk through the halls of a school, ready for the start of a new year.

Fortunately, I had something to do that day. The previous week, Kayla had called asking if I could come down to Milwaukee to spend a day with her. She didn't start classes until after Labor Day and wanted to visit with me one last time before school began. I truly believe that God put that idea into her head, because on this particular Tuesday, I needed something to do to take my mind off the reality that school was starting without me.

After Boyd left, I grabbed my iPod and my purse and headed for Milwaukee. I blasted my music the whole way down, singing loudly, not caring what other drivers might be thinking. If a sad song came on, I would skip it. Knowing how music so profoundly affects me, I didn't want anything setting me off. Although the music helped take my mind off what was happening at the high school, every once in awhile I'd look at the clock and think, Maude is speaking now, or, new staff is probably being introduced now. The activities happening at the high school were never far from my mind.

The closer I got to Milwaukee, however, the less those thoughts occurred. It was a beautiful day; the sun was shining and temperatures were forecast to be in the low 80s. I was looking forward to spending the day with my only child.

When I finally arrived, Kayla came out to greet me, giving me a big hug. She knew that this was a hard day for me and did her part to keep me in a good mood. We went up to her tiny room - it was a disaster area. A laundry basket sat on the floor, piled high with clothes.

"Are you getting ready to do laundry?" I asked Kayla.

She replied, "No, those are clean. I did laundry last week." She'd been digging through the pile for over a week, picking out the clothes she was going to wear each day. What? This can't be my daughter! I've got the laundry hung and in the closet before the warmth from the dryer has dissipated. She must take after her father.

I told Kayla to grab all her empty hangers from her closet – I couldn't handle the mess. I put the clothes on the hangers and she hung them up. There were a few clothing items strewn across the bed and desk chair, so those got hung up too. After that task was accomplished, I noticed a thick layer of dust on all of her furniture, and as I looked at myself in her full length standing mirror I could hardly see myself for all the build up. Yikes! Kayla fetched the cleaning supplies and we proceeded to clean her room. When I finished with the mirror, the difference was astounding. Kayla looked at her reflection and said, "Oh my gosh. I can see myself now! I guess I didn't realize how dirty it had gotten." I just shook my head.

After the cleaning was done, we headed out for lunch. Wanting to take advantage of the great weather, we went to a corner café located on a busy street that had outdoor seating. When we were done eating, we decided to head down to the lake to walk along the beach. It was very warm and the thought of wading in the cold water of Lake Michigan was inviting.

As Kayla and I walked down the beach, ankle-deep in the water, we talked about her classes for the upcoming semester, her roommates, and life in general. Thankfully there was no mention of my job situation. The purpose of the day was to take my mind off of that subject. After a stop at an ice cream shop and the grocery store, I headed for home, leaving Kayla with another big hug.

I didn't get home until almost 7:00 p.m. Boyd and I ate a late dinner and discussed the day's happenings. My end of the conversation was all good news – his, not so much. Boyd told me that before the convocation that morning he had briefly spoken to the other high school associate principals. They all inquired about me and wished me continued luck with my job search. As the convocation began, Boyd let me know that he almost started crying. He was thinking, "Nancy should be here." He also had a difficult time listening to Maude's speech. The reality of our situation really hit him hard that morning.

* *

Never in my wildest dreams did I imagine that I would not have a job this fall. There had been numerous administrative openings for which I'd applied, and yet, here I was without a job. I thought about the possible reasons why, after 38 applications, I'd only had two interviews. Was it because I was in my 50s? Was it because I'd been laid off after being in a district for 15 years?

Through my network I had found out that many of the available jobs this summer had been filled internally. Districts are required by law to post all open positions, even if they plan to fill them internally. I understand giving teacher leaders the opportunity to step into administrative positions within their districts. After all, that's how I began my administrative career.

School was beginning in just a few days but I was still hopeful that I would find a position. I vowed to keep applying for jobs and prayed that something good was just around the corner.

19

SEPTEMBER 2012
TWILIGHT ZONE

Federal Unemployment Rate: 7.8%
Total Number of Jobs Applied For: 48
Total Number of Interviews: 2

With Boyd gone to work every day, I had quite a bit of time on my hands. I got up before he left for the day, made my coffee, and sat in the Lazy Boy with the dog in my lap and the Today Show on the television. I felt guilty when he walked out the door while I was still home in my pajamas.

I had no motivation to do anything. All I wanted to do was sit and watch TV or do puzzle books. Ever since I was a child, I always loved doing crossword puzzles, logic problems, sudoku, and any other type of puzzle you put in front of me. When I was working I didn't have time to do puzzles; I spent my free time reading. Now, I had so much free time on my hands that I became addicted to the puzzle books.

While I sat during the day with the TV on and a puzzle book in hand, I remembered what few options daytime television offered. I needed something else to watch, something to fill the long days, something to take my mind off of my situation. While flipping through the channels one day, I happened upon the classic *Twilight Zone*. I had watched that show, off and on, since childhood and was intrigued by the stories.

A memory came to mind of a summer night, several years ago, when Kayla was in high school, still living at home. Boyd was already in bed – probably because he was getting up early the next morning to go fishing. It was a Friday night and we were looking for something to watch on TV. We ran across a *Twilight Zone* marathon. I talked Kayla into watching one episode with me - she was reluctant because it was in black and white.

After the episode ended we watched another, then another, then another. It was midnight and Kayla had to work at Kohls the next day. We decided to watch just one more 30-minute episode, and then we would go to bed. Two hours later we finally turned off the television. Kayla was now hooked on *Twilight Zone*, just like her mom.

Since I hadn't seen all the episodes, I decided to record all *Twilight Zone* shows. The show aired during the wee hours of the morning on various days. When I checked the DVR and saw that one or more episodes had been taped I was thrilled. When a marathon aired I was ecstatic! I would have more escape time that day. I know, it was sad.

My motivation to exercise was also gone. Many people, including myself, have said, "If only I had more time I would exercise." Now that I had all the time in the world, the urge was not there. For many years I got up at 5:00 a.m. to walk on the treadmill. I exercised about four days a week, before school. If I waited until after the workday, the chance of exercise was slim. I was tired and had to deal with dinner.

Walking the dog wasn't an option either. I didn't want to be spotted in the neighborhood during the day. People would know I wasn't working. So I sat on my butt most of the day, unmotivated, doing nothing.

Part of the reason I was so unmotivated was because my confidence had been shattered. Getting laid off was one thing, but the fact that I had been unable to find a job put me over the edge. I felt as if I wasn't good enough to do anything. I had applied for almost 50 jobs and had interviewed for only two positions. Depression was setting in, which was a feeling I had never experienced – at least not to this extent.

In some ways I felt as if my current life situation was a never-ending episode of the *Twilight Zone*. I wanted to go to sleep and wake up in a different place. Prayers helped, however, the knowledge that I did not have a job was constantly in the back of my mind, eating away at any morsel of positive thought I might have left.

* *

Ever since Kayla moved to Milwaukee, we would call each other a couple of times a week. Sometimes Kayla had a question for me, but most of the time, we just caught up on what was going on in our lives. Although she had already moved out when I was presented with the life-changing choice, she was very intuitive as to what I was going through.

During a weekend visit, Kayla handed me a piece of paper and said, "Mom, please read this."

I looked at the paper and noticed that she had written numerous bible verses on it. As I scanned them, I realized that they all related to my current situation. The verses talked about trusting in God, being patient in times of trouble, and not dwelling on the past. Her thoughtfulness, and awareness of what I was going through, overwhelmed me.

At the bottom of her note she had written, "Remember: Jesus loves you and will take care of you." After reading that, a feeling of relief washed over me. My perceptive daughter had taken the time to look up these pertinent verses and write them down for me. God was surely working through her. I thanked her and gave her a big hug.

I immediately went upstairs to my office and hung the note in a prominent place. Now, every time I got on the laptop, either to look for a job, or to apply for unemployment, I saw Kayla's note. I must have read it a hundred times during that difficult time in my life.

* *

As I continued my weekly job search, the number of educational openings posted online surprised me. The school year had begun, and yet, there were still a fair number of positions available. Districts were looking for administrators, math coaches, and substitute teachers. With the exception of substitute teaching, I applied for everything in which I was qualified. I was still hoping I could find a full time job for the current school year.

I had numerous websites bookmarked on my computer, including the primary educational job sites, local technical college sites, public and private four-year college sites, CareerBuilder.com, and Monster.com. I checked these websites every week. Toward the end of the month there weren't any jobs in education for which I hadn't already applied. Needing to apply for two jobs that week, I checked CareerBuilder.com for possibilities.

There was nothing in the area of education so I did a search for online writer positions. I found several openings, some in which I felt I was qualified and some not so much. I applied for an Online Technical Writer position but heard nothing from the company.

During September, I applied for a total of 10 positions – two more than required by unemployment – praying that I would get a job for the current school year. I had former colleagues calling school districts, putting in a good word for me. Still, I received no interviews.

One Monday night, Boyd returned home after playing in his tennis league with some news. He had a tennis friend, named Alex, who was a High School Principal in a city just south of us. I had applied for several jobs in that district over the past six months. Alex overheard Boyd talking with his tennis partner – a teacher who works at Boyd's school – about my jobless situation. The three men proceeded to have a conversation about me.

Boyd told Alex, "I know I'm biased, but Nancy was the best administrator I've ever had." Boyd's tennis partner, who had me as a supervisor for two years when I was an Assistant Principal at the middle school said, "I'm not quite as biased, however, I would agree that Nancy was one of the best administrators I've worked with." Alex then told Boyd to have me call him. He would be willing to meet with me, look over my application materials, and share helpful advice on finding a job.

This was very exciting news; it was another person with whom I could network. The next day I called Alex's assistant and made an appointment to see him. A few days later, we met. Alex gave me some excellent suggestions regarding how to improve my application materials. We also discussed strategies I should use in order to get an interview and we went over some common interview questions and answers.

Ninety minutes later I left his school with a renewed confidence. I couldn't believe Alex had spent so much time with me. High school principals are very busy people. When I got home I immediately made the suggested changes to my paperwork. I hoped it would result in more interview opportunities.

****

By the end of September, with no phone calls coming in for interviews, I realized I had to start substitute teaching. The thought filled me with dread. My confidence level had dropped, once again, since my conversation with Alex, and the thought of substitute teaching for the next eight months made me feel like throwing up. I cursed Maude for putting me in this situation.

Ever since school had started, Boyd and I had been having detailed conversations regarding our finances. With the exception of my unemployment checks, I had had no income since June. Despite the fact that we had cut way back on our expenses, and I was receiving unemployment, we were still taking about $1000 out of our savings account each month. That couldn't continue – I had to bring in some money. I also had to get off my butt and out of the house. I was becoming a recluse.

So I returned to the website of the school district just to the north of our home. Feeling sick to my stomach, I printed out and completed all the paperwork. The district also required new subs to get a TB test. I called my doctor and scheduled the test for early the following week. I then called the woman in charge of substitute teachers and made arrangements to deliver my paperwork.

A week later, on a brisk fall morning, I got up and dressed in a casual, yet professional-looking outfit. It was the first weekday in over a month that I was not wearing shorts, jeans, or sweatpants. Much to my surprise, it felt good to have something important to do that day.

As I drove the short distance north to drop off my paperwork, I experienced mixed feelings. Substitute teaching would be a challenge, especially since I had not been in a classroom for five years. I hadn't subbed in over 30 years and wasn't sure what to expect. At the same time, I knew I would be contributing to our household income once again.

Although the daily pay was quite a bit less than what I was making previously, every little bit would help. Boyd and I figured that I would need to sub about 10 days a month in order to avoid withdrawing money from our savings account.

The substitute teaching office was housed in the district's only middle school. As I walked into the building, I experienced an out-of-body feeling. I had been in this school only once, years before, when Kayla was in middle school. Boyd and I had attended one of Kayla's volleyball matches here. I couldn't believe that very soon I would be substitute teaching here.

The irony of the situation made my stomach turn. I had declined a full-time teaching job with my previous district because I wanted to continue to be an administrator. I didn't want to return to the classroom, and yet, that was exactly what I was doing now. To top it off, had I decided to return to the classroom in my previous district, when given the choice 18 months prior, I would have been working every day, making almost as much as I had as an administrator. I'd been in the district so long I was at the top of the pay scale. The feeling that I'd made the wrong choice once again entered my mind.

The woman I spoke with was very friendly and helpful. She checked all my paperwork and told me that the background check could take up to two weeks for the state to process. I would not be able to sub until that came through. She mentioned that the district was in need of substitute math teachers, which meant I could expect quite a few calls. There were two, relatively short online videos I needed to watch before I could start. I would then have to answer some questions about each and print certificates of completion. It was a lengthy process to become a substitute teacher.

About 10 days later I received a phone call saying my background check had come back and I was approved to begin substitute teaching. I should start expecting notification from the automated system the following day.

I was officially employed – at least part-time. It was not a job I was looking forward to doing, but at this point I really had no other choice.

I wondered, for the millionth time, how I ended up here. I asked God to please walk with me as I started down this new, totally foreign, path. I did not know what to expect in the upcoming days. I did know that I would need all the help I could get from above.

20

OCTOBER 2012
MY NEW REALITY

Federal Unemployment Rate: 7.9%
Total Number of Jobs Applied For: 58
Total Number of Interviews: 2

As much as I was dreading the start of my new, hopefully temporary, career, I was also thankful. Since I had a teaching degree, I had an advantage over many people who were unemployed – I could substitute teach. Unemployed business men and women, displaced factory workers, and people from most other professions did not have the opportunity to fill in for workers in their field. They could sign on with a temp agency, but were not guaranteed work within their own field.

With that thought, and with frequent prayers, I attempted to remain positive about my new part-time job. I reminded myself that I would be earning some much-needed income and I would have a purpose to my day.

One thing I learned at the unemployment meeting I attended in August was that if I worked part-time, I still collected unemployment. One of the questions on the Weekly Claim Certification form that I filled out online each week asked if I worked at all during the week. If I answered "yes," I would be required to provide the following information: the name of my employer, how much I made, and how many hours I worked. Using this information, the DWD used a formula to determine how much unemployment I would receive that week. Since there is a maximum amount of unemployment that can be received, working part-time and collecting only a portion of my weekly allowance extended my benefits.

* *

The school district in which I was about to begin working used an automated system to obtain substitute teachers. A teacher enters his/her absence online and the system posts the absence for all qualified subs to view. If no one takes the job within a certain amount of time, the system begins calling people to fill the absence. These phone calls take place during the evening hours, until 10:00 p.m., and then start again at about 5:20 a.m.

When my name got added to the substitute list, I didn't know what to expect. That first evening I checked the substitute website every 30 minutes or so, looking for open jobs. Very early the next morning the phone rang. Yes! I would be working that day. When I answered the phone, the automated system identified itself and the school district for which it was calling. The robot-like man's voice then told me there was an opening at an elementary school for a first grade teacher. If I wanted to accept the job I should "press one," if not, I should "press two." I was also given the option to "press three" if I did not want the job and also did not want to be called again for that day.

I pressed the number one button to accept the job.

The system gave me some more information and a confirmation number. Having thought ahead, I had placed a small pad of paper and a pen on my nightstand. I quickly wrote down the name of the school, the teacher's name, and the start and end times for the day. I got up right away and, using MapQuest, printed off the directions to the school.

I hopped in the shower, excited to have a job for the day, but also anxious. What would it be like to step into a classroom, as a teacher, for the first time in over five years? What would it be like to work with first graders? Would I run into anyone I knew? Would the lesson plans be detailed and easy to understand?

I finished getting ready, packed a lunch, ate a bowl of cereal, and quickly drank a mug of coffee. Grabbing my purse, my lunch, and a couple of water bottles, I said good-bye to Boyd and headed out the door. He was excited for me and wished me luck. I told him I'd text him if I got a chance during the day, to let him know how it was going.

It was October 4 and I was on my way to work for the first time in almost four months. More questions entered my mind as I made the 15-

minute drive to the elementary school. Where would I park? Where was the school office? Would I have enough time to read through the lesson plans and be prepared by the time the students arrived? Would I be able to handle these first graders? My nerves were getting the best of me.

Using the printed directions, I found the school with no problems. I located the office and signed in. The secretary gave me a key to the room and a "substitute teacher" badge attached to a lanyard. She told me the room number and how to get there. Quickly, I walked down the hallway anxious to read the lesson plans for the day. I opened the door, turned the lights on in the room, and immediately noticed a Smart board attached to the wall at the front of the room. Oh no. I had no clue how to use a Smart board and hoped it wasn't part of the plans for the day.

As I read through the teacher's lesson plans I flashed back almost 30 years. My teaching career had begun in an elementary school, in a second grade classroom. I remembered how quickly I had moved to the middle school level; and I remembered the reasons why. I hadn't enjoyed teaching the little ones as much as the adolescents in middle school. The memory of the little boy wetting his pants in my first classroom came flooding back. What had I gotten myself into?

Another memory came to mind as I read through the lesson plans; elementary teachers don't get many breaks during the day. Middle and high school teachers get a 45-minute period off, every day, to use as prep time. They also have a 30 to 45-minute lunch break. Elementary teachers' only down time is when their students are at their specials – art, physical education, music, etc. Fortunately for me, I would get a 30-minute break during the morning and another 30 minutes for lunch. Other than that, I would be in charge of about 26 six-year-olds for the next seven hours. Yikes!

When the first bell rang, I heard students coming down the hallway. I stood outside the classroom door to monitor the hall and to welcome the students. As the little first graders entered the room they seemed so innocent and cute, asking me my name and telling me stories as if I'd been their teacher since the start of the year. I thought to myself, "OK, I can handle this." That thought lasted about five minutes.

As I started the morning routine there were several students who kept getting out of their seats and wandering around the room for no apparent reason. I asked them, nicely, to please return to their seats. They obeyed my request, however, within a few minutes, one or more of these little scoundrels was walking around again. I tried numerous techniques to get the wandering students focused but was having little luck. My frustration level was rising by the minute and it was only 8:30.

Thankfully I got a break when the students went to choir. Before I walked them to the choir room I reviewed appropriate hallway behavior, reminding them to stay in a quiet line. Unfortunately, by the time we walked up the stairs and arrived at the door to the music room, the students were talking, poking each other, and the line was more like a crowd of people waiting to for a store to open on Black Friday. The teacher came out of the choir room and reprimanded the kids. They immediately quieted down and got back into a line. I felt as if I had been reprimanded too. I was extremely embarrassed and quickly returned to the classroom.

It had only been five years since I'd been a teacher but I felt like a fish out of water. Have I lost the ability to control a classroom of students? What am I doing wrong? Why won't these little six-year-olds listen to my directions? My positive attitude was gone and I suddenly remembered why I hated substitute teaching. Students – apparently even the youngest – will try to get away with all sorts of inappropriate behaviors with a sub.

To top off my bad mood, another teacher poked her head into the room and asked, "Are you Mrs. Chessman?"

When I replied affirmatively she told me that she recognized me from the high school in which I had previously worked; she has children who attend there. I felt obligated to tell her I'd been laid off and had been unable to find another administrative position. She responded with, "So you're subbing now?" I wanted to melt into the floor and disappear. I wanted to walk out and never return. My embarrassment hit a new high – six months ago I was a High School Associate Principal, today I was a substitute teacher.

After that, my day went from bad to worse. I struggled to keep the students on task. If I asked them to take out their markers, about half the students complied. I found myself repeating directions numerous times. Tasks that should have taken 30 seconds were taking several minutes.

I tried the proximity technique – stand close to a student who is not following directions or who is acting up. Didn't work. I tried the silence technique – stand at the front of the class with arms crossed, not saying anything, staring at the students until someone tells the others to pay attention. Didn't work. I approached students who were misbehaving and, in a hushed voice, gave them explicit directions. Didn't work. It seemed that at all times there were one or more students either walking around the classroom, crawling around the floor, or talking out. I was at a loss.

At one point, while the students were working on a task at their desks, a student said to me, "Mrs. C, Paul is under his desk crying." I had been working with several students on the other side of the room and hadn't noticed. I walked over to Paul who was, in fact, under his desk, curled up in a ball, crying. I bent down to find out what was wrong but Paul wasn't in the mood to talk. It took a couple of minutes of convincing, but Paul finally emerged from under his desk, sat down and began working. At least I had been able to accomplish one thing that day.

Throughout the day I kept looking at the clock, willing it to move faster. My patience with the little rug rats was gone. I was in a terrible mood; it took every ounce of strength I had to stay in control and not blow up at the misbehaving students. Nothing I tried was working; I couldn't imagine going through this torture every day.

About mid-afternoon, a little girl named Paige came up to me asking to go to the bathroom. In her notes, the teacher had mentioned that this particular girl had some intestinal issues and she should be allowed to use the restroom anytime she asked. I let her go and continued with the math lesson I was trying to teach. Five minutes later I noticed several of my students looking out into the hallway with their eyes wide and their mouths hanging open. I turned my head and saw Paige. She was standing at the doorway, pants and underwear around her ankles, brown stains on her shirt and hands, and tears in her eyes.

I immediately approached her, partially closing the door to block the view from the rest of the class. By the time I reached the poor little girl another teacher had arrived. She told me she would get Paige cleaned up. Thank the Lord!

As I walked back into the classroom one of the kids said, "She does that all the time." What? I found out later that Paige was a special needs student. When she returned to the classroom, in clean clothes, the students didn't say anything inappropriate to her. I was happily surprised that the little stinkers showed Paige some kindness.

The remainder of the afternoon dragged on at a snail's pace. Finally it was time to clean up the room, load backpacks, and put on jackets. When the last student walked out of the room, I sat down, completely exhausted. Once again I wondered how the regular teacher dealt with these kids on a daily basis. Was I getting too old for this or was this just an exceptionally bad group of students? How could I do this, day after day, for such a minimal amount of pay? I had already developed a renewed respect for substitute teachers.

On my drive home I remembered my first classroom experience, over 30 years ago. I thought about the second grade boy who had wet his pants, then today's incident. I had left the elementary level years ago and now wanted to leave it again – after only one day. Bitterness filled my mind. I hated my situation and hated the people who put me in it. I should still be an Associate Principal at the high school level. I had absolutely loved that job and had done an excellent job in that position. I asked God to help me get through the upcoming weeks of substitute teaching. I prayed that it would get better, because I would not last long if every day was going to be similar to the one I had just experienced.

When Boyd got home we talked about my horrible day. I was in such a bad mood I ended up taking out my frustration on him. I told Boyd that I could not sub at the lower elementary level again - it just wasn't worth it. Seeing how upset I was, Boyd agreed. I vowed to never accept a substitute teaching position if it was below the fourth grade level.

* *

The following morning I received a call from the automated system offering me a job at the middle school, teaching sixth grade math. Having taught middle school math for so many years, I eagerly accepted the job. I felt confident that my second day of subbing would go smoother than the first.

Smart boards entered the educational scene about the same time I became an administrator. Because of this, I had no clue how to operate one. Thirty years ago, when I began my teaching career, we wrote on chalkboards. By the end of the day my hands and clothes were covered with chalk dust. I used to send students outside at the end of each day to pound the erasers together, sending chalk dust flying everywhere. Students begged to do this chore and would return covered in white dust! Halfway through my career came the whiteboard. That was a welcome change, especially for math teachers, who use the board quite a bit during a lesson.

These days, many classrooms have Smart boards. The electronic boards are mounted at the front of the room, covering up the majority of any whiteboard behind it. For this reason, I had to become familiar with how to operate one.

So, on my second day of substitute teaching, the plans called for use of the Smart board. With students on the way in just a few minutes, I went looking for help. Thankfully, the teacher in the next room was willing to give me a quick lesson. I didn't even know how to turn the thing on! I found out that the computer had to be on, as well as the projector, which was connected to the Smart board. I learned just enough from the kind teacher to get me by for the day.

I was able to project the homework answers on the Smart board and then switch it over to use it as a glorified whiteboard. There were so many other things the Smart board could do, but for today I only used it for basic purposes. I was proud of myself and couldn't wait to share my experience with Boyd. He had a Smart board in his classroom and was able to use it in a variety of ways with his students.

For the most part, my second day of substitute teaching went well. I had to get after a few students for being disruptive, but I knew this age level and felt much more comfortable working with them. I also knew that when students encountered a substitute teacher, they would push the limits. I had been an educator long enough to know I would need to be firm with each class. I refused to let them walk all over me.

When I got home and told Boyd about my experience with the Smart board, he offered to give me a lesson on some of its features using the board in his classroom. I accepted his offer but told him we would have to do it when no one else was around. Regrettably, I was still uncomfortable with the thought of running into any of my former colleagues.

Boyd also had some interesting news to share with me. Another teacher at his school had approached him during the day asking how my day of subbing had gone with the first graders. She was wondering because her sister-in-law was the regular teacher in that classroom (word travels quickly!). Come to find out, the sister-in-law was also struggling with her first graders, saying it was the worst class she had ever had. That realization made me feel a whole lot better about my experience with them the day before. The behavior problems I had encountered wasn't incompetence on my part, it was the little hoodlums!

* *

The following week was slow. I did not receive a call to substitute teach until Friday. Boyd happened to mention this to his tennis friend Alex, the high school principal who met with me to go over my application paperwork. Alex told Boyd to have me apply in his school district as a substitute teacher. He offered to speak with the woman in charge of setting up subs, assuring Boyd that I would get numerous calls.

The next day I began the long process of applying to sub in the second school district. I completed much of the same paperwork as I had for the first district, several weeks prior. While on their website I noticed that the daily pay for a sub was a bit higher in this district. That was welcome news. Although I just had a background check, another one would be required before I could start subbing. That meant another two-week delay.

While I waited, I continued to work, subbing only about twice a week. I accepted several elementary positions, but keeping to my vow, none was below the fourth grade level. As I got into the swing of things, I became more confident. Although it was still a bit strange to be in a classroom again, I was helping students. That was why I entered into this profession so many years ago. It felt good to have a purpose for my day, and even better, I knew I was making a positive contribution.

* *

Each week I completed the 11 questions online in order to receive my unemployment checks. The amount was lower now that I was working part-time. I also continued to apply for at least two jobs each week. Most of the openings in education were in the Milwaukee area. Although I did not like the thought of living apart from Boyd, I needed to find a full-time job. I applied for 10 jobs in October but did not receive any invitations to interview. I was getting very discouraged with the whole job search.

It seemed as if I was praying all the time. The first thing I did when I woke up in the morning was say a prayer that this would be the day I would get a call to interview for a job. When my mind wandered during the day, it usually went to the dark place that was my current unemployment. I would say another prayer, pleading with God to get me out of this situation. And the last thing I did before I went to sleep each night was ask God to please reveal to me the new path He wanted me to travel. I was confident that He had a plan for me, a plan that would lead me to a better place. I was dealing with my current situation the best I could, but I constantly prayed for something better to come along.

There was one thing I knew for sure. The only thing holding me together during these months of unemployment was my faith. Deep down I knew that after all was said and done, I would land on my feet again, stronger and happier than I had been before. My situation sucked, but God was helping me make it through each day.

* *

Going out to eat had become a rare occurrence for Boyd and me. Before I lost my job we ate out about twice a week. Sometimes we would go to a restaurant; other times I'd pick something up on the way home from work. We also loved going out for breakfast either Saturday or Sunday morning. Now, we felt guilty spending money at restaurants and were trying not to have to take money out of our savings account at the end of the month.

One non-subbing day I decided to clean out our junk drawer in the kitchen. As I rummaged through the items, I ran across several forgotten restaurant gift cards. It was like finding hidden treasure. Then I remembered that there was a pocket in my purse in which I stuffed gift cards and coupons. I emptied the pocket and located more valuable items. I couldn't wait to show Boyd what I'd found. We would be able to go out to eat several times without spending any money.

From that day on I paid more attention to the advertisements that came in the mail. Before, I just threw them away. Now I took pleasure in clipping coupons and finding sales. When I was at the grocery store, I would stock up on sale items rather than just grabbing things off the shelf without looking at the price. With my income somewhere between one-fourth and one-third of what it used to be, saving money was a necessity.

* *

One October weekend, when Kayla was home for a visit, she took our Corolla to meet up with some friends. In an effort to save gas, she parked it in a grocery store parking lot and rode with one of her friends. At the end of the evening she was dropped off at the car and drove home.

The next day we went outside to run some errands and I noticed some deep scratches in the corner of the back fender of the Corolla. It looked as if someone had cut too close to the car and scraped it. Of course, no note had been left on our car. Kayla felt horrible about it, assuring us she had parked in the back part of the lot. The following week I took it to an auto repair shop and received an estimate of $150 to fix it. Boyd and I decided not to do the repairs at this time.

As luck would have it, within a week of the first incident, Kayla called home one evening, crying. That's the worst kind of call to receive – my only child sobbing on the phone. My mind jumped to all kinds of terrible things that could have happened to her.

Kayla explained that when returning home from dance practice, she had scraped the side of her car (an older model Toyota Prius we had given her) against the corner of the house in which she was living. She wasn't paying close enough attention and turned the car too soon. Although there was no damage to the house, the back door and back fender of the Prius were severely dented and quite a bit of paint was scratched off. She texted a picture to both Boyd and me; it looked bad. Since she would not be coming home until Thanksgiving, we told her we'd deal with it at that time.

Kayla felt sick about the mishap with her car. Sobbing, she said, "I know we don't have the money to fix the cars. I'm so sorry." We tried to calm her down, letting her know that when we were in college, we also had incidents with our cars.

This was a reminder that my unemployment was affecting the whole family. If Kayla's fender bender had happened a year ago, I'm sure she wouldn't have been quite as upset. We would have made an appointment to get both cars fixed immediately. Now, we would be waiting to repair the cars.

* *

Despite the fact that several months had gone by since my unemployment had begun, I was still embarrassed to run into people during the workday. I debated with myself about when to go to the grocery store. If I went during the day, and ran into someone I knew, they would wonder why I was there and not at work. I did not want to answer a lot of questions about my situation with neighbors, parents of former students, or retired colleagues.

I didn't want to go to the store in the evenings either, because the risk of running into someone I knew increased after the working day ended. The people who knew my situation would inevitably ask, "How are you doing?" or "How's the job search going?" The answer to both of those questions was, "Not well," and I really didn't want to get into it over and over again.

There were times when I'd round a corner with my cart, spot someone I knew down the aisle, and then quickly turn my cart around. I was getting very talented at avoiding people, although it was making my trips to the store quite a bit longer than usual. If I did encounter someone I knew, I would keep my answers short and try to escape the conversation quickly.

I found the best time to shop was on my way home from a subbing job. As a sub, I was allowed to leave the school right after the students left. Regular teachers were required to stay at least 30 minutes after dismissal time. That gave me half an hour to get in and out of the grocery store without running into anyone. How sad that it had come to this.

I was so into avoidance that I didn't even attend a good friend's husband's funeral. My former administrative assistant at the high school sent me an email informing me that Lexie's husband had died. Lexie was another administrative assistant at the high school, and I had taught her children when they were in middle school. I sent her a sympathy card and toyed with the idea of attending her husband's visitation, but in the end I didn't go. I knew there would be numerous high school teachers, students, and administrators in attendance and I was just not brave enough to attend myself. I felt extremely guilty.

The avoidance game sucked. Being embarrassed sucked. Unemployment sucked.

21

NOVEMBER 2012
HOPING TO
STRIKE IT RICH

Federal Unemployment Rate: 7.8%
Total Number of Jobs Applied For: 65
Total Number of Interviews: 3

I was now substitute teaching in two school districts, working from two to four days a week. Thankfully, during the month of November I only subbed at the elementary level one time – for a fifth grade class.

I was now receiving calls to sub at the high school level. I wasn't certified to teach that level, however, some districts weren't picky about that with substitute teachers. Having been a high school administrator, I figured it wouldn't be too bad. I was right. The students, for the most part, didn't try any funny business with me, and the teachers usually left easy-to-follow plans. After subbing at high schools in both districts, I decided I enjoyed that level the most.

As the weeks passed, I became more comfortable with my new part-time job. I still got a bit anxious on my morning drive, wondering what type of lesson I would be teaching and whether the students would be challenging. For the most part, however, it was becoming routine. There were days in which I felt more like a babysitter than a teacher. Showing a video all day or having students sit and do seatwork all day was boring. It allowed me to get quite a bit of reading done, however, I would rather be teaching.

Although not often, there were days I would come home exhausted, feeling as if most of my day was spent disciplining the students, as opposed to teaching them. On those days, I found myself looking at the clock over and over, counting the minutes until the end of the class, or better, the end of the day. Another bad sign was if a teacher from across the hall came over before the day had started saying, "There are some very challenging students in your classes today." Great – thanks for the warning.

One of the middle schools in which I subbed had a higher than usual number of students who misbehaved. They had little respect for substitute teachers and fed off of each other during class. In mid-November, I was teaching math at this middle school; the day was not going well. Students were talking, not paying attention, and needed numerous reminders to focus on the lesson I was teaching.

By the afternoon I was feeling frazzled. A young man asked, "Can I go to the restroom?"

"No, you may not," I said. "First of all, I'm in the middle of the lesson. Second, you have been disruptive the entire class."

He did not like my answer. He stood up, threw his notebook against the wall, and walked out of the room shouting, "I'm going to the f***ing bathroom, and I don't care what you think!" Whoa. I informed the office and left a note for the teacher.

To top off my bad day, one of the assistants in the office was rather rude to me when I left. There were about 30 minutes left in the day but I did not have a class during the last hour. I had written the teacher some notes, cleaned up the room, and had gone to the office to find out if there was anything else I could/should do. Typically, if a sub is not needed elsewhere, they are allowed to leave early. Well, the assistant had a real problem with me leaving early. At one point I even offered to stay – I'd go sit somewhere and read my book. She finally asked the assistant principal and he told me it would be fine to leave.

When I got home and informed Boyd about my day, he told me not to go back to that school. I had had nothing but bad experiences there. It's one thing to be treated disrespectfully by the students, but when the office staff is rude, I'm done. I was getting plenty of calls to work at other schools and didn't need the grief from this particular middle school. No matter what my circumstances were, I did not deserve to be treated disrespectfully.

Interestingly enough, I enjoyed subbing at the high school in the same district. The difference in behavior with high school students, compared with middle school students, is amazing. There was one uncomfortable aspect of substitute teaching in a neighboring town - I kept running into students from my former high school that had transferred. They would see me in the hallway or standing at the front of a classroom and would get a strange look on their faces. It was a "What are you doing here?" look.

One day I was standing in the hallway, between classes, and a student with whom I had worked with at my former high school walked by. He looked at me in surprise and verbalized the question, "What are you doing here?"

I briefly explained, "I was laid off of my previous job and have not been able to find a new administrative job, so I'm now a substitute teacher.

"Wow, that sucks!" he replied. Although I didn't say it, I totally agreed.

A few days later, I was subbing in a high school math class, teaching an upper level course. My confidence with the lesson was shaky at best, however, the teacher had left answer keys with all the work shown. Having a math background, I was able to figure out the concepts and teach the students with a modicum of comfort. At the end of one of the morning classes, a student came up to me and said, "I learned more in the last 45 minutes than I have all semester. I just wanted to let you know that." Wow. I was completely surprised. That student had made my day; for the first time in months I felt good about myself.

* *

An interesting envelope came in the mail one day – it was from Publisher's Clearinghouse. In the past I had immediately thrown all correspondence from them away, however, having seen several commercials advertising their latest offer, I opened the oversized envelope. Inside I found information letting me know that I could win millions of dollars.

All I had to do was place some stickers in the matching boxes and mail the forms, postage free, back to Publisher's Clearinghouse. I didn't even have to purchase anything.

I mailed it in.

Over the next couple of weeks we received two more offers from Publisher's Clearinghouse. I sent those in too. Now we had three chances to win millions of dollars – enough money to allow both Boyd and me to quit our jobs and never work another day in our lives. I fantasized about what it would be like to win all that money. We could pay off Kayla's school loans, pay off our mortgage, travel the world, buy a second home in Texas, and donate to charities.

We didn't win.

About the same, time the lottery reached $587 million. Boyd and I rarely bought lottery tickets. While working at the high school, if the jackpot was large enough, all the administrators chipped in a couple of dollars, in an attempt to purchase a winning ticket. I participated a few times, but not always. When the jackpot reached $587 million, Boyd and I decided to buy two tickets.

We didn't win.

* *

As the month progressed, my days became routine. Whether I was scheduled to substitute teach or not, I would get up and get ready. On occasion I would receive a late call and I wanted to be ready to work. If I didn't receive a call for that day, I would do a few things around the house and then settle down in front of the television with a my puzzle book.

This routine was so foreign to anything I'd experienced in the past. I felt guilty if I was not working, but on the other hand, dreaded getting called for elementary subbing jobs. My days at home were long and boring and I was not motivated to do much of anything. Since I rarely knew if I would be working, my morning exercise routine was nonexistent. Instead of going for a walk or getting on the treadmill I would sit on my butt all day. The lack of exercise also made me feel guilty. Needless to say, my self-esteem continued to be very low.

Sometimes, to break up the week, I would visit with my mom on a non working day. We would clean out a few dresser drawers, sort through old pictures, or organize a closet. On one of these visits, my mom handed me several gift cards worth over two hundred dollars. One was for a grocery store, another for a bed and bath store, and the third was for a restaurant. The familiar feeling of guilt overcame me for a few seconds, but I realized that mom was concerned about my situation and wanted to help. I also knew that she would not take no for an answer. I gratefully accepted the cards and thanked her profusely.

* *

One day while running errands, the "check engine" light came on in the Corolla. I didn't think too much about it and continued my errands. On my way home the car began to shake. Luckily I was close to home and made it without incident. When Boyd got home I let him know of the situation. He called the Toyota dealership and explained what was going on with the Corolla. They thought it might be the alternator and asked him to bring it in right away.

In fact, it was not only the alternator, but also the battery. This was a repair we had to make. It was going to cost us over 800 dollars. We would have to pull the money out of our savings account to pay for the repairs. There couldn't have been a worse time for this to happen.

That evening I happened to be talking to Kayla on the telephone and I mentioned what had happened with the Corolla. Knowing the car was only five years old, Kayla asked if it was still under warranty. Oh my gosh, why hadn't we thought of that?

The following day we called the Toyota dealership and inquired about a warranty. Sure enough, the majority of the repairs would be covered. Our new cost was now just under 200 dollars. Kayla's quick thinking had saved us over 600 dollars. That's my girl!

****

With Thanksgiving and Christmas just around the corner, my family began to discuss holiday plans for this year. For the first time ever, our family would not be celebrating Christmas at mom's house. Mom had been a resident of an assisted living facility for almost 10 months, and her empty house was on the market. How strange it would be to have our family gathering somewhere besides our childhood home. After some discussion, one of my brothers offered to have Christmas at his house and I offered to host Thanksgiving.

For a couple of months, there had been a promotion at the grocery store in which dollars spent there would count toward a reduction in the cost of a turkey. Since we were not going out to eat very much anymore, I was spending more at the grocery store. As it turned out, I had spent enough money to earn myself a free 22-pound turkey. I was so excited! That saved me about $30. Things like that meant a whole lot more to me now than they had in the past.

As Thanksgiving neared, department stores began advertising their Black Friday sales. In years past, these television ads evoked excitement. I thoroughly enjoyed Christmas shopping for family and friends. This year the ads were depressing. With our reduced income I knew we would not be buying many gifts. The holidays had always been one of my favorite times of the year. That would not be the case this year.

****

When Kayla came home for Thanksgiving we got our first look at the damage to the Prius. Seeing it in person, we realized the true extent of the damage. Last summer, in an attempt to save us money on our auto insurance, Boyd had raised all of our deductibles. It would cost us $500 to fix the Prius. That was not going to happen.

In an attempt to provide a temporary fix, Boyd and Kayla made a trip to the hardware store and bought a can of midnight blue spray paint. Boyd covered up the large areas of scraped-off paint on the back door and rear side panel of the car with the paint. Surprisingly, the color was a close match. Although the dents remained, the paint made the car look quite a bit better. We assured Kayla that as soon as I got a job, we would take the car in and get it fixed properly.

* *

Throughout November, I continued with my weekly ritual of applying for unemployment benefits and for two jobs. I applied for a Program Manager position at a private college, a teaching position at a local technical college, and a Director of Curriculum and Instruction position with a parochial school district. In the business world I applied for online writing and training positions. While surfing the web I ran across an opening for an E-Learning Trainer at the same company in which I had applied the previous year; the medical software company. Having been denied once, I didn't think I would have a chance at the position. Despite that thought, I applied once again.

A few days later, I received an email from the company saying, "While we won't be considering you for the E-Learning Trainer position, we would like to conduct a telephone interview with you for the position of Project Manager." Wow! That sounded like a better position than the one for which I had applied. For the first time in months, I allowed myself to feel hopeful.

I couldn't believe it. This would be my first interview in over four months. I replied to the email letting them know I would be available for a phone interview on November 27.

Immediately, I went online to find out more about the company and the Project Manager position. I knew they were located in Madison, which would mean relocation, but I needed a job. If I had to live there during the week, that was all right. Over the next couple of hours I took notes and began preparing for my upcoming interview.

On the day of the interview I did not feel nervous. I had never interviewed for a job outside of education and really didn't know what to expect. As it turned out, the woman I spoke with from the medical software company did more talking than I did. She described the Project Manager position, made sure I was willing to relocate, and asked me several basic questions. When it was over I felt as if it had gone well.

Several days later I received another email, letting me know that they were interested in having me continue on with the interview process. The next step was to take a series of skills assessments including math problems, logic problems, and basic spelling and grammar. The assessments would need to be given to me by a proctor. The company was in the process of setting something up with my local library. I should expect an email within a week or so with more details.

Once again, I was filled with hope. I felt confident that I would perform well on the assessments. It was difficult waiting to hear from them again, however, I took that time to communicate with God about this new possibility. Was this the job I was supposed to get? Was I meant to help hospital personnel instead of teachers and students? It would be a major career change for me, but the possibility brought on a real sense of excitement.

Maybe, just maybe, this would be it.

22

DECEMBER 2012
BLUE CHRISTMAS

Federal Unemployment Rate: 7.8%
Total Number of Jobs Applied For: 74
Total Number of Interviews: 4

By the time December began, the holiday season was in full swing. Houses were decorated with wreaths, lawn ornaments, and colorful lights. Red Salvation Army buckets, manned with shivering bell-ringers, were strategically placed outside all store entrances. Department store commercials filled the airwaves, advertising early bird sales and huge discounts. In the past, these things filled me with excitement and anticipation. This year it was just depressing.

Boyd and I decided that we would exchange one small gift this year. In the past we spent anywhere from $100 to $300 on each other. Not this year.

When I was in high school, back in the 1970s, I was introduced to Stephen King novels. The first one I read was *Carrie*. After that I was hooked. King has become one of my favorite authors; I own every one of his books. He had a new book that had recently come out in paperback, so I told Boyd that is what I wanted for Christmas. I was going to surprise him with a gift card for a book he could upload onto his electronic reader. That meant we would be spending about $15 for each other this year. Sad, but necessary.

Although we were keeping it simple for each other, we decided not to change things for Kayla. We typically spent about $100 on Christmas gifts for her and decided we could afford to do that again this year. So on the first Saturday of December, Boyd and I drove to Milwaukee to go Christmas shopping with Kayla.

In an attempt to get into the Christmas spirit, Boyd and I listened to Christmas CDs during the almost two hour drive to Milwaukee. Throughout the ride we talked off and on about various topics including my job situation, our finances, and the future. During a lull in the conversation, the idea of writing a book once again popped into my mind. This time, however, I had an idea of what I could write about - my journey through unemployment.

I mentioned my idea to Boyd and we talked about it for the remainder of the ride. As he asked me questions and as I put more thought into exactly what I'd write about, I began to get excited. Ideas began to pop into my head and I wished I had a piece of paper in which to make some notes. I made a mental note to get a spiral notebook from Kayla for the ride home.

By the time we reached Kayla's place we were both in a good mood and looking forward to spending the day with our daughter. We drove to a nearby mall and visited several of Kayla's favorite clothing shops. After a while, Boyd ended up finding a bench on which to sit while Kayla tried on armfuls of clothes. I sat outside the dressing room, making her show me each item so I could give her my opinion.

When we dropped Kayla back off at her place I grabbed a notebook so I could make some notes for my book while Boyd drove home. Hugs and kisses were exchanged and then we were on our way. I ended up writing about five pages of notes on the ride home. The more I wrote, the more excited I became.

I began writing this book the following week. Finally, I had something productive to do on the days in which I did not work.

* *

Traditionally, by the first week in December I would have our family Christmas letter written and ready to be stuffed into Christmas cards. For as long as I could remember we had sent Christmas cards to family and friends, including a letter and a collage of pictures taken throughout that year. This year we decided to skip that tradition. First, we didn't want to spend the money on cards and postage. Second, our year had been so depressing that a letter would have just brought people down during a season of happiness.

Throughout my adulthood, my brothers and I, along with our spouses, exchanged Christmas gifts. We would pick names so we only bought for one other person. At first it was fun buying something personal for one of my brothers or a sisters-in-law, however, it got to the point where most people were asking for gift cards. Boring. So about ten years ago we decided that instead of buying gift cards for each other, we would spend the money on people who really needed it. We began the tradition of "adopting" a needy family through a local charity organization and bought gifts for them. It was very fulfilling knowing we were helping a needy family have a better Christmas. This year, although it was difficult, Boyd and I bowed out of that tradition. We hoped that the following year we would be in a position to contribute once again.

* *

During December I applied for nine jobs. There were several public school administrator openings, two college-level positions, and a couple of openings at the preschool level. I was still required to apply for two jobs a week in order to receive unemployment checks, and I was surprised at the number of openings still available.

In early December, I received a phone call from one of Wisconsin's Cooperative Educational Service Agencies (CESA). There are twelve CESAs across the state; these agencies support Wisconsin's school districts in many capacities. In November I had applied for a Math Curriculum Specialist position with a CESA in the southern part of the state. They were calling me to interview!

When I applied for the CESA job, I never thought I'd get an interview. I lived about two hours from the main office and I figured they wouldn't consider someone who lived so far away. So when I received a request to interview, I jumped at the chance. I began preparing right away.

On December 11, I made the two-hour drive to the CESA office located just north of Madison. When I arrived, I was led to a conference room with three people present. We talked for over an hour, about the job, my qualifications, and their expectations. As the interview progressed, it became apparent that the woman in charge was impressed by my varied experience in education. She thought I would be a good fit for the position and felt confident in my abilities. Her main concern was that I would continue to look for a public school administrative position and leave the CESA position in the fall.

Although I knew I'd do a great job in the position, I also had some concerns. First, it was only part-time. Second, the salary was at a teacher's level, not an administrator's level. And third, they expected me to be in the office several times a week. That meant a two-hour drive, one way, at least twice a week. Since I would not be reimbursed for gas or mileage, I wasn't sure if the pay was worth it.

In the end, the woman said they would be completing first round interviews in the next couple of days and would be calling for second round interviews by the end of the week. She advised me to think about the position and decide if it was something I could commit to long-term. By the time I got home, I had decided that the job wasn't for me. If it had been a full-time position I would have considered it, but I just couldn't justify all the driving and gas expense for a part-time job. I discussed it with Boyd and he agreed. I ended up calling the woman back, thanking her for the opportunity, but declining a possible second interview.

* *

Ever since my phone interview in late November with the medical software company, I had been waiting, impatiently, for an email regarding the second phase of the interview process – the skills assessments. I finally received word that the assessments would be sent to my local library. Via email, I set up a date and time with the proctor at the library. Two days after my CESA interview I reported to the library to take the assessments.

When I arrived, I was handed three packets and was led to a small conference room. I closed the door, took out a pencil and a calculator, and took a deep breath. Then I carefully read the instructions for the assessments. There were three parts – mathematics, literacy, and computer language. Not only would I be graded on accuracy, but also the amount of time it took to complete each test. I decided to take the math assessment first, since I felt most comfortable with that subject.

Twenty-five minutes later, feeling confident with my answers, I completed the math test. Next, I took the computer language test; this was the one in which I felt the least amount of confidence. It was a killer test – I had to reread each question at least twice in order to fully understand what was being asked. I kept looking at the clock, thinking I was taking too much time. The pencil kept slipping out of my fingers because I was sweating. Feeling somewhat confident, I completed the hardest part of the assessment. The last part was literacy. It consisted of analogies and error-filled sentences needing grammatical corrections. I finished quickly, finding this part of the test relatively easy.

The assessments had taken me almost two hours, and it was a relief to be done. I handed the completed tests to the proctor. She put them in an envelope provided by the company and told me it would go in the mail the following day. With that, my waiting began once again. I hoped I would hear something soon.

* *

December 14, 2012 is a day no American will ever forget. That is the date of the Sandy Hook Elementary School shootings. As educators, it hit Boyd and me hard. Although all schools train for these types of situations, most people believe it could never happen in their community.

When I returned to substitute teaching the following week, I was nervous. As I walked into the different classrooms each morning, I immediately surveyed the space and looked for a place for the students and me to hide. I also made sure the door was locked. Despite the fact that I kept the classroom door open throughout the day, knowing the lock was set made me feel better. What a shame that educators across the nation, as well as students and parents, have to worry about such things.

Although I had only been subbing for about two months, I began to receive notifications from the automated system letting me know that teachers were requesting me to be their substitute. It felt great knowing that I was wanted and appreciated. I hadn't felt that way in my former school district for years. My confidence, which had been so badly beaten down, was given a slight boost each time I received one of these requests.

****

With the holidays upon us, and sweet treats in abundance, I tried to make more of an effort to get on the treadmill. In all the years I've used the treadmill, I've walked in the morning before school. So, my exercise took place at 5:00 a.m.

When I was working full time, and had a daily routine, it was much easier to motivate myself to exercise. In my current situation, I usually didn't know if I was going to be working that day until somewhere between 5:30 and 6:30 in the morning. On occasion I would get up, walk on the treadmill with the phone nearby, then shower and get ready. Unfortunately, many times I would not get a call to sub, and then I'd be all dressed up with nowhere to go. That got old really fast.

Despite all that, I was exercising several times a week. I began to notice that when walking at a faster pace the walking belt would slip. It happened randomly and took me by surprise each time it occurred. It was a bit scary because it felt as if I was going to lose my balance and fall. I mentioned the slipping belt to Boyd. We knew we could not afford to buy a new treadmill and we didn't really want to pay someone to fix our 12-year-old machine.

Fortunately, I was able to find the user's guide for this particular treadmill online. I printed a couple of pages of information on how to fix a slipping belt. As I read the instructions, Boyd worked on the treadmill. Together, we were able to fix the problem ourselves, at no cost. I wonder if we would have dealt with this problem the same way several years ago when we both had stable employment.

* *

Miraculously, the week before Christmas I received two phone calls offering job interviews. The first to call was the medical software company. The woman told me I had done well on the skills assessments and an interview was set for the first week of January. It would take place in Madison and would be a full day interview, including a tour of the facility, lunch in the cafeteria, plus interviews with several different people. I was told to look for an informational packet in the mail with more details. Although the idea of a full day interview was a bit intimidating, I was ecstatic!

A day or two later, I received a phone call from a school district about 30 miles north of my home. I had applied for a Dean of Students position in an elementary school. It was only an interim position; the current dean would be on maternity leave for 12 weeks. Even so, I accepted the offer of an interview. It would take place the day after my interview in Madison.

* *

Winter break began several days before Christmas. Kayla had finished her last exam but, because of her job at Kohls, would only be able to come home for a few days. The holidays were obviously the busiest time for department stores, and Kayla was lucky to get a few days off.

We took part in the same holiday traditions as always, however, there was heaviness in my chest throughout the festivities. I was supposed to have a job by now. Our financial situation should have been back to stable. It was impossible for me to enjoy the holidays with my joblessness still hanging over my head.

Christmas Eve arrived, and with it the usual lasagna dinner and opening of gifts. Boyd and I watched Kayla open the presents from us and marveled at how excited she got, even though she had picked most of them out herself! We opened our one small gift from each other and several that Kayla had gotten us.

I don't consider myself materialistic, however, this was a lean Christmas. We usually had many more gifts to open. While we cleaned up the wrapping paper and ribbons, sadness overtook me. This is not how we were supposed to be celebrating Christmas. The thought that haunted me on a daily basis surfaced once again; I should have a job by now. If I did we wouldn't be in this situation. My eyes welled up with tears; I tried to hide it from Boyd and Kayla but they could tell something was wrong.

I attempted to explain why I was upset. They told me that the most important thing was that we were together for the holiday. They were right, of course, but losing that horrible feeling in my chest was easier said than done.

23

JANUARY 2013
WHEN IT RAINS IT POURS

Federal Unemployment Rate: 7.9%
Total Number of Jobs Applied For: 81
Total Number of Interviews: 7

The new year began on a high note for me. Not only did I have two scheduled interviews, but I also received two more phone calls requesting interviews. One of these calls came from a small school district about 20 miles from home. I had applied for a high school principal position there in early December. The other call came from a school district a bit further away. They had an interim middle school associate principal opening that began in late January and ran through the end of the school year. With four interviews scheduled for early January, I felt very confident that by the end of the month I would be employed.

On January 2nd, I packed a bag and headed for Madison for my interview with the medical software company for a Project Manager position. Due to the fact that this company conducts interviews with people from all across the country, they put all candidates up in a hotel the night before the interview. I presume this is to guarantee on-time arrival – or they just want to give a good impression. Whatever the reason, I enjoyed the evening at a hotel, ordering dinner from room service, and doing some last minute preparations for my interview.

The following morning I checked out of the hotel and, leaving with time to spare, drove to my interview. I arrived at 9:30 and checked in with the receptionist. The full-day interview was to begin at 9:45 so I sat in the waiting area until someone came for me. While I waited, I people-watched. Every person that walked by looked like a kid! I had heard that this company likes to hire younger people, but I was hoping that, despite my age, I'd make a good enough impression to get hired.

A young man from the human resources department approached me, introduced himself and took me upstairs. I was given a folder containing my schedule for the day and some information about the company. There were several other people in the HR waiting room and I soon realized that there were six of us being interviewed for various positions within the company. After looking over my schedule I also realized that we would be in groups for some of the activities.

First on the agenda was a group tour and company overview. For the next 45 minutes we walked through several buildings and received information about the various departments. This was followed by a software demonstration. We were taken to a conference room and were shown exactly how the medical software worked and how it helped hospitals and clinics across the country.

The next part of the interview involved speaking with a current Project Manager who would give us some insight into exactly what the job entailed. There was one other candidate who was applying for a PM position, so the two of us were led to a room for the overview. While we were talking I found out that the other candidate was a senior in college. Oh my! My competition was my daughter's age!

Next we were taken to the college-style cafeteria for lunch. I was impressed by the numerous food choices and by the size of the cafeteria. One wall was made up of floor to ceiling windows, providing a fantastic view of the beautiful countryside that surrounded the grounds. There were hundreds of people enjoying lunch and talking animatedly. As we ate and talked, I looked around the room. Once again it struck me that there were very few people in the room who were over the age of forty.

Following lunch, I was taken to a small conference room for my 10-minute presentation. When I was initially contacted for this interview, I was told that I would be doing a short presentation similar to a demonstration speech. I figured they want to find out if a candidate is able to explain a process effectively. As the three participants entered the room, my nervousness increased, however, I had practiced the presentation numerous times and knew I would do a good job. Once I began, my nerves all but disappeared. When it was over I felt as if I had done an excellent job.

After my presentation I was taken to the human resources office for an actual interview. I spent about 30 minutes answering questions. Next came a case study interview. I was escorted to yet another room where I was given time to read over a case study and take notes. When the interviewer returned, he asked me numerous questions about the situation in which I had just read. Most of the questions were along the lines of, "How would you handle this person?" or "What would you do to solve this conflict?"

Having spent five years as a school administrator, I had experience with many personalities, conflicts, and difficult situations. Relying on my experiences, I answered the questions to the best of my ability. I left the room feeling, once again, as if I had answered the questions competently.

One last interview was left – this one was the Project Management interview. Another young man took me to a room and asked me questions pertaining directly to the PM position for which I was applying. I was able to answer his questions with confidence. He then took me back to the human resources office for a wrap up.

As I left the building, walking toward my car, I felt very hopeful. I had spent over five hours participating in the various components of the interview. During my two-hour drive home I called Boyd, then Kayla, then my mom, letting them know that the interview had gone well. I felt confident about the possibility of obtaining this job. It would mean moving to Madison and living apart from Boyd during the workweek. Despite that unappealing aspect, I thought this position would be a perfect fit for me. I had been told that I would be contacted, either way, within a week or two. That meant more waiting. It seemed that waiting was all I had been doing for months and months.

* *

The following day I made the 30-minute drive north for my second interview of the month. This interview was for the interim dean of students position at an elementary school. When I arrived at the school I was led into the principal's office. Very quickly it became apparent to both the principal and myself that I was overqualified for the job. The main responsibility of this position was student supervision. The majority of my day would be spent either outside during recess times or in the cafeteria supervising the lunchroom.

As unpleasant as that sounded to me, I gave my best throughout the interview. I needed a job, and if that meant standing outside, freezing, for a couple of hours a day, I would suck it up and do it. Before I left, the principal told me that, within a week, she would be selecting two finalists. She would check their references and then make a decision. More waiting.

* *

My next interview, for a high school principal position, took place on a Monday evening. I spent hours researching the school and practicing possible questions and answers that might come up during the interview. Although I felt prepared, my nerves were at an all time high as I walked into the school.

The interview panel consisted of nine people, including school board members, administrators and teachers. For almost an hour I answered questions from each of the panel members. Some of the questions were easy to answer but, as always, I was asked several unexpected questions. I answered these to the best of my ability, hoping I was making a good impression.

As I drove home I began to second-guess some of my answers. This happened after almost every interview. For days I replayed their questions and my answers in my head, thinking of better ways in which I could have responded. Hindsight is always 20/20.

* *

As I began to prepare for my fourth interview, as always, I went online to research the school district. The position for which I was a applying was an interim middle school assistant principal. When I received the phone call from the principal of the school, asking me for an interview, he had explained that the person was to start in late January and work through the end of the school year. The job would be posted again in the spring as a permanent position. He also told me that he had checked my references with my former school district and that I came highly recommended. He was very interested in speaking with me. I found out later that James, my former boss and administrative colleague, was the person who had recommended me to this principal.

When I applied for this position back in December, it was mainly because I needed to apply for two jobs a week in order to collect unemployment. I never thought they would call me for an interview. Up to that point I was only receiving about one interview for every 18 jobs for which I applied. My confidence level had been as low as my mood.

Thinking that the drive to this school district would take about an hour and a quarter, I decided to check online. Much to my surprise, the district was two hours from my home. Once again I had to make a decision. If I landed this job I would have to relocate; driving four hours a day to and from work was not an option. The position was interim with no guarantees of employment for the following year.

Boyd and I discussed the situation, weighing the pros and cons. Would it be worth it for me to move into an apartment for several months if I was offered this job? Did I want to live in a place where I knew no one? At least when I applied for jobs in the Milwaukee area, I knew Kayla would be close enough to visit with on occasion. In the end, since the position was only temporary, we decided that I wouldn't interview for the position.

This time it was me doing the "thanks but no thanks" phone call. Knowing I had three other options for employment had helped us make this decision. Surely one of those options would result in a job for me.

* *

In mid-January, Kayla came home for a long weekend. Her second semester classes would be starting soon which would make coming home for a visit more difficult. Having Kayla around was a good distraction for me. My situation was always lurking at the back of my mind, but having Kayla home made life a bit more bearable.

While she was home we checked online to find out how much we owed for tuition for the upcoming semester. Although she had financial aid, which brought the amount down, we still owed thousands of dollars. Kayla also let us know that she would be doing an internship during the summer. She would be able to earn credits for this experience – credits she needed in order to graduate – which meant more of an expense for us.

After Kayla headed back to Milwaukee I wrote the tuition check and transferred money out of our savings account to cover the check. It was then that I realized the money we had put away for Kayla's college costs was almost gone. We had only enough to cover this semester and her summer internship credits. There was no money left to pay for her senior year.

With me earning so much less now, we hadn't been able to put money away each month, as we had been doing for many years. A feeling of panic ensued. What were we going to do? I said a prayer to God asking Him to help us with this financial problem. I had to get a job soon so we could start saving for Kayla's college expenses again.

* *

A week had passed with no word from any of the employers with whom I'd interviewed. I finally received an email from one of my references letting me know that he was getting reference calls about me. That was good news; prospective employers usually check the references only of people they are considering for the job.

Two weeks after my interview for the interim elementary dean of students position, I received an email saying they had chosen someone else. I knew I had been a finalist because my references had been checked. In the end though, they decided upon the other finalist. I was overqualified for that position, so I wasn't totally surprised that I didn't get the job. Disappointed, but not surprised.

One job gone, two others still a possibility.

Within a day or two of my first rejection came the second. I received a phone call regarding the high school principal position. I was told that the job was given to another candidate, "But thanks for taking the time to interview with us!"

Ugh. Only one job opportunity left.

I hadn't heard anything from the medical software company for two weeks, so I decided to give my recruiter a call. I left a message on her answering machine and hoped for a speedy reply. Five days later, with no returned phone call, I called again, leaving another message. The following day she called back letting me know that they were in the process of checking references.

Debra, my former supervisor, emailed me the next day to let me know the company had contacted her. Finally some progress was being made, and a small sense of hopefulness returned. I knew some organizations took quite a while to make a decision after interviews were conducted, however, my experience had taught me that the longer the wait, the worse the outcome.

Another week passed with no news. It had been a month since my interview and I was losing hope quickly. I finally emailed my recruiter asking if a decision had been made about the Project Manager position. She called the following day letting me know that I did not get the job. Although deep down I knew that would be the outcome, receiving the final "no" was still hard. And, knowing that the job went to someone who hadn't even graduated from college yet didn't help matters.

Strike three.

* *

Unfortunately, the bad news didn't end there. A friend of mine who still worked at my previous school district told me that the district had hired a half-time administrator to help with the workload at the high school. What? They had gotten rid of me and within six months had added back a half-time administrator? I didn't think it was possible, but even after I was no longer employed there, I received another slap in the face.

I remembered the conversation I had had with Debra almost a year ago in which I had approached her with the idea of a 50/50 administrative position. The district administrators had used part of that idea – although I was not part of it.

If any school districts in the area got wind of this, it would look very bad for me. They might wonder why I was not asked to return for this position. It could place major red flags in front of my name on job applications.

My stress level went up another notch.

I don't think that Maude had any idea of how her actions were affecting people. If she did, she might think twice about some of the decisions she was making. Or, maybe she did know how she was hurting people, and simply didn't care. I remember a former colleague of mine saying, "It's a good thing Maude doesn't have any of her own children, because she would eat her young."

* *

It was about this time that I realized I would most likely be substitute teaching for the remainder of the school year. That thought was absolutely depressing. Even though I had "good" days, I was really not enjoying my job as a sub. It wasn't fulfilling and I felt as if I had no real purpose in life. I wasn't helping students and staff in the same ways in which I had for so many years.

With our money woes always at the front of our minds, Boyd and I began to discuss other ways to reduce our expenses. Interest rates had dropped and we talked about refinancing the house – again. During the 13 years in which we had lived in our home, we had already refinanced on two occasions. Hoping for good news, we called our banker. He ran the numbers and let us know that, if we refinanced, we could save about $200 a month on our mortgage payment. It would extend our loan by three years, but at this point we needed to cut our expenses. A closing date was set for the following month.

There was another bit of good news for us regarding our finances. Two of our three cars had been paid off for years, so we only had one car payment. That that loan would be paid off in April. We would be saving another $350 a month.

We decided to put that money into our savings account and earmark it for Kayla's senior year college expenses. It wouldn't add up to the total amount we would need, but it would definitely help.

* *

The emotional rollercoaster ride I was on hit some major highs and major lows in January. With several interviews, I had been certain that I would be employed by the end of the month. When that didn't happen I went through a very depressing time, feeling unworthy and unfulfilled, with my confidence level at an all-time low.

I felt as if my life was out of my control. With white knuckles I was holding onto the rollercoaster safety bar for dear life, while it sped around corners, threatening to fly off the track. I was at the mercy of the coaster and gravity, hoping for a rapid end to the nightmare ride.

24

FEBRUARY 2013
IT'S NOT WHAT YOU KNOW
IT'S WHO YOU KNOW

Federal Unemployment Rate: 7.9%
Total Number of Jobs Applied For: 87
Total Number of Interviews: 7

On Friday, February 1st, I drove down to Milwaukee to visit with Kayla for the day. She had called several times during the week and, although she hadn't said anything, I could tell something was bothering her. When I arrived at her place and walked into her bedroom I noticed that her boyfriend's maroon football jersey was not hanging on her wall anymore. I turned to her questioningly and, by the look on her face, realized what was wrong.

Without either of us saying a word we embraced and shared a long hug. Kayla started to cry. I wasn't sure who had done the breaking up, however, I knew the relationship had ended. Kayla filled me in on what had happened and by the time she had finished her explanation I knew she felt a bit better. Although she was the one who broke up with him, she was still heartbroken. At that moment I was so glad I had made the decision to visit Kayla that day. It always helps to have your mom there to help you get through the difficult times.

We spent the day together, going out for lunch and doing some grocery shopping. When we returned to her apartment and began to unpack her groceries, a couple of her roommates returned home. For the next couple of hours, I was able to forget about my situation and actually have fun hanging out with Kayla and her friends. They shared some interesting college stories with me – some made me laugh and some surprised me. In many ways college was the same as it had been when I had attended over 30 years prior!

* *

The following week I was called to sub in a middle school math classroom. The teacher was attending a funeral out of town and they needed a sub for three days. The assistant principal at that middle school, Jason, was the husband of one of my book club friends. We had known each other for years, due to the fact that I had taught with his wife before they had even met. He was also very familiar with my current situation.

Jason stopped by to see me during my lunch break to let me know that there was a 6th grade teacher who was pregnant and would be needing a long-term sub from March 20 through the end of the school year. She taught 6th grade science and language arts. Jason wanted to know if I would be interested in the long-term position. I immediately told him that I was interested and thanked him for thinking of me.

The following day I found out that I had been approved to fill the long-term position. I knew Jason had put in a good word for me and that his recommendation was the reason I obtained the job. At least temporarily, God had answered my prayers.

Having this new position meant that not only would I be working full time again, but I would also be making more money. Since I would be doing lesson plans, grading papers, and assigning grades, my daily pay increased. Although science was probably my least favorite subject to teach, I was ecstatic about this opportunity! No more wondering whether I would be working each day, and no more worrying about what type of lesson plans and/or students I would encounter. I would finish out the school year in one position, at one school, with the same students each day. My friend had come through for me!

* *

Kayla called me a few days later, crying. She told me that she had been at work and had seen a woman in a red winter coat. For a moment she thought the woman was me and had gotten excited. When she realized it wasn't me she became sad and wished I was there with her. She said she didn't know why she was crying, even though we both knew she was still getting over her boyfriend break-up and needed her mom. In an attempt to help her feel better, I told her that I had broken down with my mom in August when I told her about the unemployment meeting I was required to attend. Sometimes we just need our moms…

* *

Once I landed the long-term substitute teaching position, I called the unemployment office to inform them of my full time job. I found out that I could have stopped applying for two jobs a week several months ago. What? The rule is that after you work part-time (32 hours a week) for four weeks in a row, you no longer have to apply for jobs each week. They also told me that once my full time position started I would no longer need to apply for any more jobs. I obviously would not be collecting unemployment while working full time, so I would not be going online to fill out the weekly claim form anymore.

One other piece of information I found out was that I only had about three weeks of unemployment benefits left. There was an option to apply for emergency funding that would extend the benefits, however, I was hoping that I would not have to go that route.

Toward the end of the month we refinanced the house. We had set the date strategically so that we would miss two house payments. We were hoping to put that money aside to use for Kayla's fall tuition. We were still in a tight spot financially. Although I was working full time, the pay was considerably lower than what I had been making the previous year. Cutting back had become our new way of life.

25

MARCH 2013
BACK TO TEMPORARY
FULL TIME EMPLOYMENT

Federal Unemployment Rate: 7.7%
Total Number of Jobs Applied For: 89
Total Number of Interviews: 7

In early March, one of our middle school teacher colleagues decided he had had enough of the system, and Maude. He abruptly quit. A Happy Hour was planned to wish him well in his future endeavors. I debated whether or not to attend. I was doing such a great job playing the role of a recluse that my first instinct was to stay at home. I was very apprehensive about the whole thing because I would be socializing with the teachers and administrators from the school in which, just a few years earlier, I had been an assistant principal.

Hallie, the associate principal with whom I had worked at this middle school for two years, was driving over an hour to be there. I lived five minutes from the party venue and figured that if Hallie was making the effort, I should too. I really wanted to see Hallie and the rest of my former colleagues, however, I knew the uncomfortable questions were going to be asked, the looks of pity were going to be given, and my feelings of inadequacy would surface. I was also worried that one or more of the central office administrators might be there and I certainly did not want to see any of them.

As Boyd and I drove to the party, I mentally prepared myself. I knew that the people I was getting ready to encounter respected me and wanted the best for me. Their questions would not be for obtaining gossip or to make me feel bad. I knew they were genuinely concerned for me. As much as I told myself all of that, I still felt great apprehension.

With my stomach in my throat, we walked to the patio to join in the celebration.

Things went pretty much as I had expected. Many people came up to talk to me since I had been in hiding for so long. Questions were asked, condolences over my situation were shared, and, yes, the looks of pity were on several faces. More than anything, my former colleagues let me know much they missed me, and reminded me of what a fantastic job I had done at the middle school. Many told me there would be something better for me in a different school district. That comment fit right in with my belief that God had a plan for me.

In the end, I was glad I had gone. I talked to Hallie for quite a while. She was now a central office administrator in a school district that was about an hour and a half away. She loved her new job and told me that she finally felt appreciated for her knowledge and insight in working with teachers and administrators. I was genuinely happy for her because she deserved to be recognized for her talents.

* *

Toward the end of March, I started my long-term subbing position as a 6th grade science and language arts teacher. It felt good to be in a routine again, getting up each weekday morning and going to work. Knowing more money was going to be coming in was also a perk.

The first week in "my" new classroom was great! That's what teachers call the honeymoon period. I was getting to know the students and they were getting to know me. They were adjusting to how I ran things as opposed to the teacher they had grown to know and appreciate since last September. The students were well behaved that first week.

The second week of subbing did not go as smoothly as the first. I had been waiting for it to happen; several students tested me by acting out. I had to speak with these students about their behavior and threatened to call their parents (a great technique as long as you carry through with the threat when necessary!). By the end of the week, I had regained control of the classes.

My days became busy again. Since I knew I was working every day, I got back into getting up early and walking on the treadmill each day. I was very busy with lesson planning, grading papers, and all the other tasks required of teachers. I thanked God often for this opportunity to work with children again, and for the financial boost.

* *

March is when jobs for the following school year start to pick up on the employment websites. Although I was busy with work, I took the time to check the websites for openings in our area. Since I was no longer collecting unemployment, I was not required to apply for two jobs each week. Despite this fact, I was still very motivated to find an administrative position for the following school year.

Unfortunately there were very few administrative openings listed at this time. I applied for only two jobs in school districts within 40 minutes from our home. One of those jobs was in the school district in which I was currently subbing. My hope was that I was building a good reputation with the district and that working in the district would help me to get a foot in the door. Having to go through the process of filling out an online application, waiting for a phone call, preparing for an interview (or more likely, not getting an interview at all), and waiting for another phone call, was getting really old.

* *

Boyd and I were talking one day and the topic of our return to Texas came up. When we moved north to Wisconsin, we knew that we would eventually return to Texas. The original plan was to work in Wisconsin until we retired, then move back to the Austin area.

When Boyd began talking about retirement, somewhat jokingly, a few years ago I told him that he had to work until Kayla graduated from college. Since we were paying her tuition and most of her room and board, minus student loans, we needed his income. When I lost my job, his income became even more important.

Kayla had one year of college left, and was also talking about moving south. Texas was one of several places she was considering. Boyd was definitely looking at the 2013-14 school year as his last. The thought of Boyd retiring from teaching when I was, for all intents and purposes, unemployed, made me nervous. He assured me that he would be working, full or at least part-time, after his retirement. He was burned out with teaching and had several ideas about other employment he could pursue.

We decided that after the school year ended we would take a trip down to Austin and San Antonio. It had been awhile since we had been to Texas and we wanted to visit some of Boyd's family, and our friends. Because her internship didn't start until later in June, Kayla was able to join us. We hadn't had the opportunity to spend an extended amount of time with her in several years, so we were very excited about this news! Since there were three drivers, we decided to drive straight through. That would save us having to spend money on a hotel on the way down and on the way back.

Although the thought of spending any money on a trip was worrisome, we wanted to visit friends and family that we hadn't seen for years. We also planned to look at several areas in which we might want to live. With the possibility of a return to Boyd's birth state in the future, we needed a plan.

26

APRIL 2013
MORE OF THE SAME

Federal Unemployment Rate: 7.6%
Total Number of Jobs Applied For: 91
Total Number of Interviews: 7

Although I was enjoying the substitute teaching, I came home exhausted. I hadn't spent all day, full time, with students for six years. I was bringing work home just about every night. There were lesson plans to develop and papers to grade. As an administrator I would also come home tired, but it was a different type of exhaustion.

After only subbing full time for only two weeks, the district in which I was working had their spring break. Boyd had already had his spring break, and we didn't have any extra money, so we hadn't gone anywhere. I used my time off to diligently start my job search once again.

As I scoured the different school districts' websites I was disappointed at how few openings existed. I applied for only two jobs, both further away from home than I preferred. The process of filling out the applications, writing cover letters, and electronically sending in all necessary paperwork took its toll on me. I began to feel that old familiar stress again.

On my 20-minute drive to and from school each day, my mind would inevitably turn to my future joblessness. My stomach ached on a daily basis. With every thought of the job search, my heart would pound in my chest. I did not want to go through another spring and summer like last year. I thought about the countless hours I had already spent looking for a job, rarely getting an interview.

Also on my mind was the thought of going back on unemployment. There would be no income from me during the summer months, which meant I would need to collect money from the government again. That was just one of many depressing thoughts that entered my mind on a regular basis.

* *

On a Friday in mid-April, I met up with some of my administrative colleagues from my former school district for a happy hour. They told me that there were three administrative openings in their district. People were jumping ship. Things had gotten pretty bad for teachers and administrators under Maude's leadership, and many people were looking elsewhere for jobs. Although I did not see it that way at the time, my friends told me that I was one of the lucky ones. They once again told me that they truly believed there was something better for me out there. I prayed they were right.

After that happy hour I was depressed for the entire weekend. Hearing about all the administrative job openings in my former school district got me worried. I knew that human resource personnel from school districts in the vicinity spoke with one another. If any districts were interested in me, they would surely call my former HR boss. Human resource personnel know of the openings in nearby districts. They might wonder why, having spent 15 years in my former district, I was not being considered for any positions there. Even if Maude wasn't blackballing me, the fact that I was not being considered for any jobs in my former district would not look good. Stomachache, pounding heart, sleeplessness…

* *

On April 16, Boyd woke up with shortness of breath and chest pain. With his heart scare occurring just over a year ago, we were not going to take any chances. We both obtained subs for the day and I took him to the emergency room. He ended up spending two days in the hospital. The doctors blamed the incident on anxiety. Hmmm, I wonder what caused that?

* *

In late April the weather finally began to warm up. I was able to get some yard work done and Boyd and I did our semi annual garage cleaning. It felt good to be working outside once again.

About this time we decided to get my Corolla fixed. Boyd worked his magic with the man at the repair shop and it only cost us $125. Once again I thanked God for another blessing He had sent our way.

It had been over a month since I had put in an application for any and all administrative positions in the school district in which I was substitute teaching. I checked their web site almost daily for any administrative openings to be posted. Nothing.

I once again lay in bed at night thinking about my situation and losing confidence in myself. I felt as if I had no chance at any administrative position. I felt worthless. Depression set in again and was not going to go away for quite awhile.

27

MAY 2013
ANOTHER DISAPPOINTMENT

Federal Unemployment Rate: 7.5%
Total Number of Jobs Applied For: 93
Total Number of Interviews: 7

As the end of the school year approached, I had mixed feelings about the upcoming summer. It would be nice to have some time off, however, if I did not have a full time job lined up for the fall, it would be the third summer in a row in which I would be job-hunting. My goal was to have an administrative job before the school year ended. That gave me five weeks.

I hoped I had done enough in the school district in which I was substitute teaching in order to land an administrative position there. I had made a good impression with two principals in the district – Alex, a high school principal, and the middle school principal who was currently my boss. I had earned respect from teachers and office staff for the subbing I had done in their schools, and I had a letter of recommendation from my current principal. Surely those things would at least earn me an interview.

There were only two openings in that district during the entire month of May. Both positions were for assistant principals at the high school level. No problem! I had been an associate principal at the high school in my old school district for two years. One of the openings was at Alex's school. He was Boyd's tennis buddy who had helped me with my resume and cover letter. I was confident that I would be interviewing for the position at his school.

I actually called Alex a week after I had applied to find out how far along they were in the hiring process. He checked on his computer and told me that I had made the first cut. What that meant was that I had scored high enough on the "perceiver" to be considered for an interview. A perceiver is a timed, online "test" that asks questions about your personality and your leadership style. Fortunately, I had answered the questions in a way in which they approved. So now I just had to wait for a call to interview.

* *

Kayla came home for Mother's Day. While she was home, we took the Prius in for an estimate. It was going to cost $700 to fix the car. We told the repairman that we would be bringing it back the following month.

Once again, we received an envelope in the mail from Publisher's Clearinghouse. I filled out the required paperwork and sent it in. You can't win if you don't play! About the same time, the lottery reached almost $600 million. Boyd and 65 other teachers from his school pooled their money and bought tickets. Some of the teachers joked about how awesome it would be – if they had a winning ticket – to walk into Maude's office, all together, with their letters of resignation in hand. As I already mentioned, Maude's approval rating was at an all-time low with teachers and administrators.

No luck was had on either attempt at winning big.

* *

On May 23rd, Boyd ran over his cell phone in the driveway. We found out that it would cost $150 up front for a new phone, plus $15 a month for 16 months. He had to have a cell phone, so we bought one.

On May 27th, Kayla called. She had gotten into a car accident. It was not her fault, however, there was damage to her front bumper. She was upset and mad that another driver had caused the wreck. We told her not to worry and that we would have the collision repair shop look at it next month when the previous damage was being repaired.

On May 28th, I found out that interviews had taken place the previous week for the two high school assistant principal positions for which I had applied. All my hard work, and all the connections I had made in the district, once again, had gotten me nothing.

Another week from hell…

28

JUNE 2013
CONSIDERING A MAJOR CHANGE

Federal Unemployment Rate: 7.5%
Total Number of Jobs Applied For: 108
Total Number of Interviews: 8

During the first week of June, we took Kayla's car to the repair shop to get it fixed. The cost ended up to be $700, as the estimate had stated. The only good news was that the repairman was nice enough to pop out the front bumper at no cost.

The school year ended on June 5th, and so did my long-term subbing position. My goal of having a job by the end of the school year had not materialized, and once again, I was not bringing in any money. With a guilt-filled heart I called the unemployment office to find out what I needed to do at this point. It had been months since I had applied to receive funding and I wasn't sure what needed to be done in order to start it up again.

The woman I spoke with was very rude. She acted as if I was stupid or ignorant. By the end of the call I was almost in tears. I told her that I was hoping to get a job soon so that I would only have to be on unemployment for a few weeks. Maybe she was so rude to me because she was having a bad day. All I know is that she made me feel very inadequate; a feeling that was becoming all too familiar.

* *

The day after school let out, I got on the computer to look for a job. I applied for a middle school assistant principal position in a town about 40 minutes north of our home. A former colleague of mine from my old district had recently taken a job there. I called her up and asked her if she would put in a good word for me. She immediately agreed to help me out.

During our conversation she filled me in on some personnel changes in our old district. Troy had left the district! He had been named as the superintendent in a nearby town. Good for him, I thought! He needed to get out from under Maude and have freedom to run his own district in a positive, professional manner. My friend also told me that the man who had gotten the assistant principal position at my old middle school (the one who still didn't have his administrative degree!) had been moved to the high school. That meant there was an opening at the middle school in which I had worked as an administrator for two years.

Later that day I told Boyd about the opening at his school. We looked at each other, both of us knowing the questions running through my mind. Do I dare apply for the job? Do I really want to work for Maude again in that toxic environment? Would I just be embarrassing myself by applying for a job in my old district?

In the end, I decided to apply for the job. I had nothing to lose, and really didn't care what they thought of me. I even called the principal at the middle school. She had only been a colleague of mine for one year and I didn't know her very well, but she was Boyd's boss and had had several conversations with him regarding my situation.

When I spoke with the principal she seemed to be genuinely interested in what I had to say. I made my case, using the same arguments I had used with Troy two years earlier. I reminded her that I had been an assistant principal at that school for two years, I knew the staff members quite well, and was familiar with the school's schedule, philosophies, and behavioral procedures. At the end of our conversation I asked her if she would put in a good word for me with the central office administrators. She agreed to do so.

Although the conversation went well, I did not hold out much hope for an interview. Honestly, I wasn't even sure if she would follow up with my request. It really didn't matter. I had to apply for the position. Whatever the outcome, it would speak volumes as to the mindset of my former district regarding my reemployment with them.

* *

Every few weeks, the topic of our possible move back to Texas was brought up. Boyd was serious about retiring from teaching at the end of the 2013-14 school year. Kayla would be graduating from college at the same time, and my future employment was yet to be determined. Due to all of these factors, we decided that we were definitely going to make the move.

We were not sure where Kayla would end up after graduation, however, we hoped she would decide to move to the Austin area. Austin was still on her list of places to move after graduation, but so were several other places. She knew we wanted her close to us after our move, but, as hard as it was, we had to let her figure it out on her own. I now was adding a prayer about Kayla moving to Austin along with my prayers of finding a job.

Knowing we would be returning to Texas the following year, a thought entered my mind. Why don't I apply for jobs in Texas now? It seemed as if no district in Wisconsin wanted me, so why don't I try school districts in the Austin area? It would mean moving away from my family and having living costs in Texas. There would be flights to pay for so I could return for holidays, and it could be very lonely for me being alone and so far away from everyone.

While knowing all the negatives in my plan, I was so desperate for a job that I was willing to go for it. I brought the subject up with Boyd. He did not want to be separated from me for almost an entire year, and did not like the idea of me being alone and so far away. After discussing the plan further we decided that I should investigate the openings in the Austin area districts and apply for the ones that interested me. It would not be an ideal situation, however, if it meant full-time employment, it might be worth it.

I prayed to God to give me guidance in this endeavor. Maybe this was His plan for me. I couldn't imagine that He would want to our family separated, however, I was running out of options.

* *

The week after school ended we loaded our luggage into the Suburban and made our way to Texas. As always, the 22-hour drive (not including stops) started out with excitement and anticipation. We took turns driving, navigating, and sleeping. By hour 12, the three of us had talked about everything there was to talk about and were tired. Darkness was almost upon us and the amount of time each of us could drive was getting shorter. Hour 18 brought on grumpiness and the need for some decent sleep – sleep that involved actually lying down on a bed!

As we got closer to our destination we all began to perk up. The end was in sight and so was a comfortable hotel room. We spent the next week in San Antonio, visiting Boyd's family, and in Austin visiting our friends. We celebrated my birthday and our 27th wedding anniversary while in Texas.

On our anniversary, Kayla presented us with a gift. Tom Petty was going to be in concert at Milwaukee's Summerfest at the end of June. She had bought us tickets for the concert! Boyd and I are huge Tom Petty fans and this gift was a total surprise. Kayla apologized that the tickets were toward the back of the arena (because that is all she could afford) but that didn't matter to us. We were going to see Tom Petty – a real treat. This event was something we would not have spent our money on, which made it even more special.

Our last day in Texas was Father's Day. We slept in knowing we had the long drive home that evening. After brunch, we decided to go through some model homes in an "active retirement community" we were considering just north of Austin. The community was for people 50 and older, and offered hundreds of clubs and activities.

Boyd and I had dreamt of living in a community like this for several years. We wanted to retire in a place with people our age and with lots of things to do to keep us active. We both still played tennis and Boyd golfed. Even though Boyd would not be entirely retired, and I was still years from retirement, we met the age requirement and decided to check out the homes and the community.

As we walked through the model homes we discussed the pros and cons of each. Kayla gave us her opinions too. We started out with the smaller, less expensive homes. The prices were higher than we had ever paid for a home, but we were just looking. Just dreaming of life in this community.

The fourth house was a step up – in square footage and in price. We walked in the front door and through the foyer. As we approached the living room/kitchen area I stopped and said to Boyd and Kayla, "I want this house! This is my dream kitchen!" Now, my idea of a dream kitchen is probably different than most other people. The kitchen was the perfect size, with lots of cupboard space, granite countertops, stainless appliances, and a decent-sized pantry. The best part, though, was that it was totally open to the dining room and living room areas. There was a counter and raised bar that faced out to the living space. It was perfect!

I ran my hand across the bar then turned in a circle to take in the main living area. The dining room was a bit smaller than the one in our current home, but I knew we could make it work. One wall in the living room featured three large windows. I pictured in my head how I would arrange our furniture. I fell in love with the house without even seeing the rest of it. I had always wanted a home with a kitchen that was open to the rest of the family area, but had never been lucky enough to have that. The other homes we had owned throughout our marriage were very nice, but this was the one I pictured in my head when thinking of our retirement home.

We picked up the information sheet to find out the square footage, and more importantly, the price. Yikes! It was considerably more expensive than any other home we had ever purchased. My hopes were dashed. We absolutely could not afford this house. My dream home was out of our reach.

Despite my disappointment we toured the rest of the home. It was lovely. I could picture Boyd and myself living very comfortably in this three bedroom, two bathroom home. We toured the rest of the models, each one getting bigger and more expensive. It made me feel a bit better about the home I had fallen in love with, however, I knew we could never afford it. With Boyd retiring from teaching next year, and my job situation up in the air, I accepted the fact that we would never own this home.

After our visit to the retirement community we grabbed a quick dinner and began the long drive back to Wisconsin. The entire way back I kept picturing that home. I wanted to remember every glorious detail.

* *

The following week was not a good one. After the high of being on our first vacation in over two years, I struggled to get through each jobless day.

I immediately began the massive job of applying for administrative jobs in Texas. The system for online applications was a bit different, and because I was starting from scratch, it took me many hours to complete the process. I applied for nine positions in the Austin area and two more in Wisconsin. That brought my total to 15 job applications filled out for July. Surely something would come of it.

When I was not applying for jobs, I had nothing to do, and all the time in the world to do it. Working around the house became my distractor. I cleaned out drawers, closets, the pantry and any other cluttered place I could find. Anything to take my mind off of the fact that after 13 months, I still did not have a job. My prayers increased once again.

Shortly after our return from Texas, I got a call from the school district in which my former colleague worked. They wanted to interview me for the middle school assistant principal position! My friend had come through for me!

I spent three days preparing for the interview. I would go into a room by myself and practice possible questions, giving the answers out loud. I found that technique to work better than just thinking about the answers in my head. Speaking the answers aloud helped me in my delivery and fluidness. I also went online to learn more about the district and the school by visiting their websites. This was my first interview in five months and I wanted to be fully prepared.

The last week of June was another rollercoaster ride. On the 27th Boyd had his annual performance review with his assistant principal. When he returned home, I could tell by the look on his face that things had not gone well. For the second year in a row he would not be getting a raise.

During the previous school year, no teachers in the district received a raise (although somehow there was enough money to give Maude and the other central office staff a pay increase). This year, against the advice from the state of Wisconsin Education Association, the district used the new evaluation tool to determine teachers' salaries. Teachers had to earn a certain amount of points on their evaluation in order to receive a pay increase. Boyd had just missed the cutoff for a raise. He found out later that he was not alone. Many of his colleagues also did not receive pay increases. Despite that bit of knowledge, Boyd and I wondered if he was being targeted because of me.

That same day, we attended the funeral of one of my aunts. She was my dad's sister and also my godmother. She was in her 80s and had lived a long and happy life, but it's still hard to say good-bye for the final time.

My dad's side of the family is large and we saw many aunts, uncles, and cousins that day. The subject of work always comes up and, once again, I found myself embarrassed to discuss my joblessness with my family. I knew my extended family members were not judging me, but I still felt worthless, having to discuss for the hundredth time, the fact that I still did not have a job. The only good news I had to share was my upcoming interview.

That interview occurred the following day. During the 40-minute drive, I once again, reviewed typical interview questions. Although I felt confident and prepared, that nervous feeling was lying just below the surface. Someone once told me that feeling nervous was a good thing. I hoped they were correct!

I arrived at the central administration office and walked into the building. After checking in with the receptionist I was instructed to sit and wait to be called. This wait is the hardest part of any interview. And the longer the wait, the more nervous I got. I checked my purse to make sure my cell phone was turned off. Then, in an attempt to calm myself, I took a few deep breaths. The importance of doing well in this interview weighed on my mind.

Eventually, I was led to a room in which about 10 people were seated around a large table. I sat at the only open spot, at the head of the table. I looked around and smiled at everyone. As they went around and introduced themselves I began to calm down. There were principals, teachers, and school board members ready to ask questions.

The interview consisted of only 11 questions. Many of them were situational, "What would you do if …" As I answered each question I brought up personal experiences that pertained to the situation. This was important to do in order to let the panel understand that I was well rounded in my administrative experiences. I also remembered to smile and inject humor when appropriate.

When the questioning was over I asked a couple of questions of them. They told me that second interviews could possibly occur the following week. No decision would be made until after the week of July 4th.

On my drive home I reviewed the interview in my head. I felt as if I had answered the questions thoroughly and to the best of my ability. As I reflected on the experience it occurred to me that it had been very impersonal. There had been no follow-up questions after my answers, and few indications from the people involved as to how they perceived my answers. In past interviews, the questioners would smile, nod their heads, or even comment after I gave an answer. That was not the case in this interview. Maybe this district always ran their interviews this way. Whatever the case, I knew I had done my best and hoped to be receiving a phone call for a second interview in the next few days.

* *

That same evening was the Tom Petty concert in Milwaukee. As soon as I got home from the interview I changed clothes and we headed out the door. We wanted to get down to Summerfest a few hours before the concert so we could enjoy the some of the local bands that would be playing on various stages on the fairgrounds.

On the drive down Boyd and I discussed my interview. I shared my perception of the impersonal atmosphere with him. We concluded that every district has a slightly different method of interviewing candidates and that I shouldn't worry. So I put it out of my mind, as much as possible, and we changed the subject.

We stopped by Kayla's place for a short time before heading to the fairgrounds. She shared with us the best place to park for the least amount of money. After catching up with Kayla, and thanking her again for the Tom Petty tickets, we headed to Summerfest.

The main stage at Milwaukee's Summerfest seats thousands of people. A roof covers the stage and a large portion of the seats. The remaining seats are behind the covered area and are not protected from the elements. That's where our seats were located.

The good news was that several giant screens had been placed strategically around the stage for those of us in the back to get a close-up view of the band. The bad news was that a storm was blowing in. As we entered the venue it began to rain. We found our seats but then quickly moved up to stand under the last bit of roof available behind the covered seats.

Many people were taking refuge there. We stood for quite awhile, leaning on the railing, able to stay dry. Security people occasionally walked past and told us that when the concert started we would have to sit down. We were just hoping that the storm would pass soon.

As luck would have it, the rain stopped just before the concert began. We went back to our sopping wet seats, brushed them off as best as we could, and sat down. Tom Petty and his band entered the stage and began to play "American Girl." The crowd went crazy!

It wasn't more than 10 minutes into the show that Boyd and I looked at each other and began to laugh. The smell of marijuana filled the air. We hadn't experienced that odor since the 1990s! We had not attended many concerts since Kayla had been born.

The concert was phenomenal. Tom Petty sang all of his greatest hits and then some. We sang the words along with the band, cheered, clapped, and had a great time. For those few hours I was able to forget about everything and just enjoy the moment.

* *

Our trip to Summerfest was on a Friday. The weekend that followed was worrisome for me. I prayed to God that I would get a phone call for a second interview. July was just around the corner and my time to find a job for the upcoming school year was quickly running out.

29

JULY 2013
MY PRAYERS INTENSIFY

Federal Unemployment Rate: 7.3%
Total Number of Jobs Applied For: 139
Total Number of Interviews: 8

Following a weekend filled with worry, Monday arrived. As Monday morning became Monday late afternoon, with no call, my mood darkened. I got on the computer to check out other job openings, then checked email, and finally, with nothing better to do, logged onto my Facebook account. As I was scanning the most recent posts I ran across something that totally changed my mood. One of my Facebook friends had posted the following quote, "Don't worry about anything; instead, pray about everything; tell God your needs and don't forget to thank Him for His answers. If you do this you will experience God's peace, which is far more wonderful than the human mind can understand." It was a verse from Philippians 4.

As I read the verse my stress melted away. Although I have a strong faith, sometimes I need a reminder that God is always looking out for me. I felt as if God had placed that verse on Facebook Himself for me to see!

I realized that I might not hear any news from the school district until after the holiday, but instead of stressing out all week I decided to hand the situation over to God. If the job were meant to be, it would happen. Worrying about it for a week would not change the outcome. So I let it go and kept myself busy for the next week.

Boyd and I went strawberry picking on Tuesday morning. In the past, this event was a major tradition for my family. My mom, sister-in-laws, and our children would drive to a "pick-your-own" strawberry patch to pick (and eat!) strawberries. We would grab as many crates as we wanted to fill and hop on the hay-filled trailer to get a ride to the spot that was being picked that day.

By the time we were done picking, our shoes, and our fingers, were stained red. If it were a hot day we would all be sweating and tired, our back's aching. After the strawberries were weighed and paid for, we would drive over to my mom's house and make batch after batch of strawberry freezer jam.

Unfortunately, those days are over. My mom's health prevented her from coming along anymore. As the years passed, and our children grew up, fewer and fewer family members participated in the strawberry picking. So this year it was just the two of us. Kayla was living and working in Milwaukee, so I talked Boyd into coming to help. Strawberry picking was not a chore I wanted to do alone. After the picking, I spent the next two days making freezer jam and pies.

My next chore was cleaning the windows. We had put new windows on the entire house a few years back and had upgraded to the kind that could be cleaned, inside and out, from inside the house. This came in handy considering we had a two-story home. Despite that fact, this was one of my least favorite jobs to do. It took me two days to complete the task.

Here and there, throughout the July 4th week, I found time to write. Even if it was just making notes or doing rereads, it was one of the few things I was doing that made me feel like I was accomplishing something. My writing and my chores helped keep my mind occupied. It was a good distraction from my worries surrounding my job search.

* *

I received an interesting phone call the following week. Hallie called to let me know they were looking for a principal at the lone elementary school in her district. She was wondering if I would be interested in applying for the opening. I thanked her for thinking of me, but told her of our plans to move to Texas the following summer. I did not want to commit to a job in her district if I could only do it for one year.

Hallie had done so much to help me when I was a beginning administrator. She had taught me so many valuable lessons, and above and beyond that, we were friends. I felt an obligation to let her know of our plans.

* *

No call ever came for the second interview I was so hoping for. I did not call them either, which I sometimes did following an interview. It wasn't until the 16th of July that I finally received an email from the district letting me know they had chosen someone else. So much time had elapsed that the email, and its contents, was not a surprise. It was just another disappointment in an ever-growing list of disappointments.

In the meantime, I applied for 23 more jobs in Texas and 8 in Wisconsin. The process of applying for jobs had become so mundane and tiresome that I dreaded it. So much time and energy was being put into my job search with so few interviews. I felt as if I was just wasting my time.

The thought that I might be substitute teaching for a second year in a row began to creep into my mind. It kept me up at night and entered my thoughts during the day. I told myself that I would go insane if I had to sub for another school year.

* *

My former administrative colleagues scheduled another happy hour in mid July. We met at a local bar and grill to relax and catch up on everyone's latest news. At this particular happy hour I found out that there were five lawsuits against my former school district. Several retired administrators initiated one of the lawsuits, and another was from current teachers. I've already mentioned that many people were not happy with the way Maude was running the district. The lawsuits were proof of the dissatisfaction.

Someone suggested that I bring a lawsuit against the district. I had not been given a realistic reason as to why I had been laid off. There was also the fact that Troy had told me straight out they would not consider me for any administrative or teaching position in the district. The "confidentiality" reasoning that they had given to me would not even apply if I were a teacher in the district.

On my drive home I thought about the lawsuit suggestion. If I were to pursue a lawsuit it would probably result in my name being put out in the local newspapers. That would not be a good thing since I was still looking for a job in the area. And, honestly, I just wanted to move on and not deal with Maude ever again.

* *

As I was looking online for a job I ran across an opportunity to go to various school districts to promote/sell a math program. They offered a two-hour webinar to learn about the product and the position. I had never worked in sales, however, I had listened to many sales people over the years who had come to my school district to sell their product. I was comfortable speaking in front of groups of adults so I thought I'd watch the webinar and find out what it was all about.

With a feeling of excitement I started the webinar. The math program they were selling looked great! I had taught math and worked with math teachers throughout my educational career, which made me extremely knowledgeable about the subject.

About half way through the webinar I found out that there was a training program that I would be required to attend at my own expense. The training cost $1500, but I would also have to pay airfare and hotel. The next training session wasn't until September, and it was in Atlanta. I also found out that I would have to recruit school districts myself. That was a big surprise. By the end of the webinar I realized that this would not work for me. Once again, my hopes had been dashed.

* *

Knowing that we were moving to Texas in a year, I began to go through closets and our storage shelves in the basement. We would need to get rid of many of our things because homes in Texas do not have basements. We had two large shelving units that Boyd had made that were loaded with boxes and bins. There were holiday decorations, extra kitchen items, things we were saving for Kayla, and so much more.

We also had a huge walk-in closet in the basement that we used for our off-season clothes. The finished part of the basement had furniture, pictures on the wall, a television and a small bar refrigerator. We were planning on giving the furniture to Kayla (wherever she ended up!) but had many items that needed to go.

I put larger items on Craigslist and began to put smaller items in a corner of the basement for a rummage sale. It was a huge task! Boyd helped me go through boxes so we could decide together what to keep and what to sell. Toward the end of July, Kayla came home for a weekend. We went through her bedroom closet and dresser looking for clothes to sell or give away.

In the past, I put off such a mundane task as long as possible. Now, I actually looked forward to it. Anything that helped me forget about the constant unknowing, the countless rejections, the heavy pain in my chest, and the never-ending stomachache, was welcome.

* *

On a rainy morning, I drove to my doctor's office for my annual physical. As always, they took my blood pressure before I saw the doctor. It was 146/82! That was the highest reading I had ever had. My blood pressure was usually around 120/75. I blamed the reading on the stressful situation I was currently experiencing.

Later that same day I received an email from one of the districts in which I had substitute taught the previous year. They wanted to know if I planned on subbing there again this school year. Just reading the email gave me a sick feeling in my stomach. I really did not want to sub again for another whole school year, but if I did not find a job that is exactly what I would have to do.

Thank goodness I received the email after my doctor's appointment. I can only imagine what my blood pressure would have been had I read the email before I saw the doctor.

July was over, and I still did not have a job. The pressure was building again. I had applied for 31 jobs this month and had heard nothing from any of them. My praying increased as I, once again, asked God to guide me in the right direction. I knew that He had a plan for me, it was just so difficult waiting for it to happen.

30

AUGUST 2013
THE WAIT IS FINALLY OVER

Federal Unemployment Rate: 7.3%

Total Number of Jobs Applied For: 157

Total Number of Interviews: 9

During the first week of August I received a letter from the unemployment office. It said I was required to attend a meeting on August 14th. This is the same meeting as I attended last year. It obviously was an annual requirement. Memories of last year's meeting flooded my brain. The embarrassment and feelings of inadequacy I had experienced rushed back into my head. I would have to go through all of that again.

For days I perseverated on the upcoming meeting. It consumed every thought of every day. The only positive was that it motivated me to work even harder to find a job. During the first two weeks of August I applied for 18 more jobs. Eleven of those applications were for school districts in Texas and three were in Wisconsin. The administrative job openings, at least in Wisconsin, were drying up.

Four of the jobs for which I applied were outside of school districts. One position was for a Regional Operations Manager and Trainer for a local homebuilder. Another job was with a software company. They were looking for a Technical Training Specialist. Being an educator, I figured a training job would be right up my alley. I also applied for two consultant jobs related to education.

The fact that the school year was starting in less than a month did not escape me. My stomach hurt on a daily basis and my stress level was through the roof. Between thinking about the upcoming unemployment meeting and the possibility that I would be substitute teaching for another year, I was in a constant bad mood.

It seemed as if I was talking to God every hour. I constantly reminded myself that I was a strong woman and could get through anything. There was a plan for me and I just needed to be patient. Have I mentioned that patience is not one of my stronger qualities?

* *

On Friday, August 9 my cell phone rang. I noticed that it was Hallie calling me. I figured she was calling to see how I was doing. After we exchanged the usual pleasantries Hallie told me something that would change my life.

Hallie's school district had been looking for a new elementary principal for months. She had called me in July to ask if I would be interested in interviewing for the position. I had declined, due to the fact that we would be moving to Texas the following summer. Hallie's district had conducted two rounds of interviews during the summer and had not been happy with any of the candidates.

With the school year quickly approaching, and Hallie being one of the best problem-solvers I have ever known, she had proposed an idea to her superintendent, Adele. Hallie's idea was quickly accepted by Adele, and by the school board. They were now looking for an elementary principal to fulfill a one-year contract.

Hallie explained to me that the former principal had left under unfavorable circumstances. The morale at the elementary school was at an all-time low, and the rules and procedures for teachers, students, and parents had not been consistently enforced. She told me that she thought I would be the perfect person to come in and make some necessary changes, while at the same time raise the morale at the school.

Hallie asked me if I would be available on Monday, August 12 to make the 90-minute drive to her school district so that I could interview with several district personnel. I could hardly believe what I was hearing. My ears were actually ringing and my head was swimming. Of course I was available on Monday! We set up a time to meet and said our good-byes.

The first thing I did was to tell Boyd the news – I had an interview in Hallie's school district! The second thing I did was get online to learn as much as I could about the school district. I found out that the district had one elementary, one middle, and one high school. It was located in a relatively small town near Lake Michigan.

Although it was a small town, the elementary school had over 600 students. It housed students from kindergarten through fourth grade. There was one administrator at the school – just the principal. The thought of that was a bit daunting, however, I reminded myself that I had five years of experience as an administrator. I also knew that if I were fortunate enough to get the job, Hallie would be only a phone call away.

Trying to hide my excitement, I called Kayla and my mom to let them know of the most recent development. I told them I wasn't getting my hopes up too much, but that I was cautiously optimistic about the upcoming interview. Both reassured me that I would do a great job and both said they would be praying for me.

* *

When I woke up that Monday morning, the sun was shining and I was in a good mood. I had spent most of the weekend preparing for the interview. I left the house early, as always, with Hallie's directions on the seat next to me. The 90-minute drive was pleasant, much of it through the beautiful Wisconsin countryside.

The interview was to be held in Adele's office, which was housed in the same building as the high school. I found the school, parked my car, and walked in with time to spare. The receptionist had me take a seat and the uncomfortable waiting began.

Hallie came out first to greet me and told me it would be a few minutes before the interview would start. Eventually she took me to the superintendent's office and introduced me to Adele and the director of special education. My first impression was that both were strong women, like Hallie and myself.

The interview was less an interview and more an explanation to me about the current environment at the elementary school. Adele did most of the talking, letting me know of her concerns and asking me a few questions. I felt very comfortable throughout the interview, partially because Hallie, a friendly face, was there, and partially because I liked the women with whom I was conversing. My initial impression was correct. These three women knew what was best for the students and teachers in their district and knew how to accomplish their goals with compassion. I liked what I was hearing and made my case as to why I would be the right person to take over as the elementary principal.

While we were talking, it occurred to me that, more than anything else, these women wanted to meet me and get a feel for me. I knew Hallie had spoken very highly of me and had given them assurance that I would be the right person for the job.

Before I left they told me that, with the beginning of the school year quickly approaching, a decision would be made soon. I shook their hands, thanked them for the opportunity, and walked out feeling very excited.

On my drive home I replayed the hour-long conversation in my head. I knew that if I was chosen I would be able to help the students and staff at that elementary school. Boyd has shared with me that my administrative style is one of getting the hard things done while at the same time being compassionate with the people with whom I work. That analysis fit right in with what I had observed during my interview.

Hallie called me later that day to let me know I had done a great job. She said that Adele would be making a decision very quickly. She gave no hint as to whether I had the job or not, which was the right thing to do, and I did not ask.

* *

The following day Adele called, offering me the job. I was elated! After 14 months of unemployment and over two years of applying for jobs, I was finally employed. My prayers had finally been answered. This was God's plan for me.

Relief washed over me. The tightness in my chest let loose and my 14-month stomachache finally abated. A feeling of euphoria arose in me. The stress was finally over. The wait was finally over. My prayers had finally been answered.

This wasn't going to be just a job – it was going to be a challenge. I would be the principal of a large elementary school that was in disrepair. I was being brought in to improve the morale, the attitudes, and the day-to-day challenges every school faces. There was much work to be done, but I had every confidence that I would succeed. So had God. This was His plan for me. There was a need and I was placed there to help. I couldn't wait to start!

I called Hallie and thanked her profusely. She had worked her magic so that I could get this position. As I remembered, Hallie had told me of a high school assistant principal opening in her district two years earlier when I was first looking for a new position. She then had let me know of the elementary principal opening the previous month. I guess the third time's the charm – the one-year opening fit right in with my plans and also helped her school district. It occurred to me that Hallie had been looking out for me since my situation had become public knowledge, over two years ago. Hallie was my hero!

I shared my excellent news with family and friends. They were all extremely happy for me. My start date would be the following Monday, August 19.

* *

After receiving the job offer I called the unemployment office. I wanted to let them know that I had obtained a job and would not be attending the dreaded meeting, which was to occur the following day. The timing of my new job came just in time for me to be able to skip the unemployment meeting. I said a thank you prayer to God for that small miracle!

This new position also meant I would no longer have to apply for unemployment benefits. I was grateful for that – I had never felt comfortable getting help from the government, even though I was told it was my right. As it turned out, I had received about 11 months of unemployment income. It had helped us get through the last 14 months, and for that I was grateful.

* *

On August 19, I moved my things into my new office at the elementary school. After that, I hit the ground running. There were staff and students to meet, meetings to plan, a building to become familiar with, and so much more. I was in my element and loving every minute.

God had come through for me, as I knew He would. Life was good again!

EPILOGUE

Once I received the job offer, life became a welcomed whirlwind. Since my new school was about 90 minutes from home, Boyd and I decided I should look for an apartment about halfway between our home and my new school. Having a 90-minute commute twice a day was not going to work for me. I would stay in the apartment during the week and come home on the weekends.

We put our home up for sale in October and it sold quickly. Right after Christmas, Boyd moved into the two-bedroom apartment with me. We rented two storage units to hold all of the things we couldn't fit in the apartment. It was a bit cramped, moving from a 2,300 square foot home into a 950 square foot apartment, but we knew it was only temporary.

My new position as the principal of a large elementary school kept me extremely busy. At the beginning of the school year I spent quite a bit of time getting to know staff, students, and parents. I made it a priority to make each staff member realize they were a valuable contributor to the school. My goal was to get the morale and school climate back to the high level it had been in the past.

Throughout the school year I worked on student truancy, playground issues, parking lot and parent pick-up issues, and much more. I truly loved being around the young kiddos. I received numerous hugs on a daily basis! Although I knew I was only going to be at this school for one year, I wanted to make a lasting contribution. I was just so grateful to have a job that I loved; a job that I knew I was good at; a job in which I knew I was making a difference.

About halfway through the school year Hallie dropped by my office. Since we were working closely on many matters related to the elementary school, this was a regular occurrence. She told me that she had just returned from an administrative conference. While at the conference she had run into Troy. Troy had gotten out from under Maude's supervision and was a superintendent in a neighboring district.

Hallie mentioned to Troy what a great job I was doing as the elementary principal. Much to her surprise, Troy responded, "Of course she's a great administrator!" When I heard that, I realized that my perception of Troy as being Maude's "bad news delivery boy" had been correct. He did respect me as an administrator – even though he couldn't show that while he was my boss.

In March, Adele stopped by the elementary school, as she did often. She came into my office and sat down. Unlike my former district, when a central office administrator walked into my office in my new school district, I felt comfortable and at ease. She told me that she was extremely happy with the job I was doing. Every time she walked into the school she could feel the positive vibe from staff and students. Adele then asked me if my plans to move to Texas were still on. Although I was on a one-year contract she was hoping I would reconsider and stay on as the principal.

Adele's words meant so much to me. It had been so long since I had received a compliment for my work in the schools. Actually, I realized that numerous people – teachers, staff members, Hallie, other central office administrators, parents, and students – had told me how much they appreciated me. My confidence and self-worth, which had been so badly beaten down in my former district, had been totally restored.

Hallie, and some of the staff at the elementary school had also approached me, hoping I would reconsider my move to Texas. I actually spoke to Boyd about staying another year or two. I loved my job and the people with whom I was working. In the end, we decided to stick with our original plan. Kayla had finally made the decision to move to the Austin area with us. We were ecstatic about that news!

During the spring of 2014 my mother's health began to decline quickly. She fought a great battle, but died on April 10, two months before our move to Texas. Our family was devastated, however, we knew she was no longer in pain and she was with dad again. That thought comforted us.

The school year ended and I said my good-byes to all the people who had supported and appreciated me. That same month, Boyd officially retired from teaching. There was a huge celebration party for him, and several other retirees from his school, at a local establishment. I happily attended that party.

We had one last rummage sale, donated many items to charity, and packed up the rest of our things. We visited with my brothers and their families one last time, extending an open invitation to visit us in Texas anytime.

On June 30, 2014, we began our two-day drive south to Texas. Kayla would spend one last summer in Milwaukee and would move to Texas in late August. We had arranged a rental home in which we would live for several months. The reason we were renting was because we were waiting for our new home to be built. Our new home. The home with my dream kitchen. Yes, we were able to afford the house that I had only dreamt of a year ago.

When I reflect on everything I endured for over two years, I realize that, if it weren't for Maude, the choice she forced me to make, and my fateful decision, we would not be where we are today. I am a true believer in the "everything happens for a reason" adage. The hell Maude put me through landed me in the best possible place.

Besides the support of my family and friends, the main thing that got me through those awful two years was my faith. I prayed so often and so hard during that difficult time, it resulted in a strengthening of my faith. Although this experience was an extended hell, I knew deep down that God had a plan for me. He doesn't always answer our prayers immediately, but He always answers them. He wanted me to be the principal at the large elementary school in the small town, even if only for one year. He wanted me to make the move back to Texas in 2014. The timing of that allowed us to buy our dream home, live in a community we love, and also to live in close proximity to Kayla.

My prayers since our move have mostly been prayers of thanks.

Oh, one more thing. After moving to Texas in July, I found a job within a month, and began working again in August.

ACKNOWLEDGMENTS

I would like to acknowledge my parents, Fran and Bev, for raising me to be a strong woman with a strong faith. Although neither will ever read my book, I felt their presence with every word I typed. To my brothers and their families, I thank you for always making me laugh, even when there seemed as if there was nothing left to laugh about.

To my colleagues and friends from my former school district, thank you for helping me through the hard days. Without your constant encouragement, those two years would have been very lonely. A special thank you goes out to my book club buds. You ladies were always there for me, ready to listen and offer your love and prayers.

A very special thank you to Sara Bork, who spent many hours helping me with the editing of this book. Your advice and suggestions were spot on.

Finally, a huge thank you to Boyd and Kayla. You not only lived this nightmare with me, but also supported me while I took on the enormous endeavor of writing this book. Throughout it all, you two were able to lift my spirits, raise my self-confidence, and most of all, just be there for me. To borrow an adage my mom often used to say, "I love you to the moon and back."

CPSIA information can be obtained
at www.ICGtesting.com
Printed in the USA
BVOW06s0206100218
507495BV00005B/153/P